Praise for *The Value of Core Values*

I thought I understood core values. After reading *The Value of Core Values*, I realized I didn't fully understand what core values meant for my company. This book helped me see the difference between a marketing tag line based on words and core values that are truly integrated into the life of my business. More importantly, by implementing the Five Keys described in this book, we have become a values-centric organization where my leadership team is driving a change in our culture. Now, we not only say it, we live it throughout our organization!

~ Patricia Dominguez, CEO/President
Triage Partners

The Value of Core Values is an insightful, compelling read that challenges anyone leading a business to integrate key ideals into daily operations to fully and harmoniously realize the potential of the organization and its individuals.

~ Kristen Allman, Of Counsel Constangy
Brooks & Smith, LLP

This book provides the 'why' and the 'how' to create a values-centered culture in any organization.

~ Matthew Kelly,
New York Times bestselling author of *The Dream Manager*

The reality is that every leader and organization operates according to a set of values. *The Value of Core Values* challenges you to address a set of critical questions: Do you know what those values are? What do your employees, customers, suppliers, and others think those values are? Are those values the ones for which you want to be known and which lead to success? This book contains a series of engaging, practical stories of real leaders who have answered these questions and successfully managed to shape the culture of their companies based on their core values. Most importantly, it lays out a path for those who would follow their examples. The *The Value of Core Values* should be required reading for leaders at all levels in both the public and private sectors.

~ Carl Bennink, Ph.D., Senior Consultant
Professional Staff Associates

The message of core values should be the drumbeat by which all leaders manage. This book shows you how.

~ Glenn Henderson, CEO
AFC Worldwide Express

I could not put it down! Every leader of an underperforming company should read this.

~ Mark Galvan, Business Coach and Mediator
Resource 2 Management

America was built on core values but in today's mixed world they need to be focused on more than ever. *The Value of Core Values* gives us a good tool to understand and rebuild what many organizations have lost.

~ John Grant
Florida State Senator (Ret.), Attorney at Law

Using excellent and practical case studies, *The Value of Core Values* presents how to realize the value of living core values in a tenacious, well defined and structured way. We the readers get a clear appreciation of the rewards of living and running our businesses directed by the core principle of doing what is right.

~ Imelda K Butler, Chairperson
Odyssey Transformational Strategies

The Value of Core Values:
Five Keys to Success through Values-Centered Leadership

By Lisa Huetteman
Published by:
Fidelis SDG, LLC
2505 Mason Oaks Drive
Valrico, FL 33596

Copyright © 2012 by Lisa Huetteman

Hardcover ISBN: 978-1-61434-470-4
Paperback ISBN: 978-1-61434-471-1

Internet website addresses and references offered as a citation and/or source for further information may have changed or disappeared after the publishing date.

First Edition, 2012
Published in the United States of America

The Value of Core Values

*Five Keys to Success through
Values-Centered Leadership*

Lisa Huetteman

About the Author

Lisa Huetteman has over 30 years' executive experience in both Fortune 500 and small business development. She is currently an executive coach, consultant, author, and speaker. Lisa is co-founder of Black Diamond Associates <u>www.the-black-diamond.com</u>. She lives in Valrico, Florida with her husband, two daughters and their Bichon Frisé named Chloe.

Table of Contents

Foreword

By Pat Williams

From the time I played on my first athletic team at the age of twelve, sports have been a passion and focus of my life. Since 1968, I've served as general manager for National Basketball Association teams in Chicago, Atlanta, and Philadelphia, including the 1983 World Champion 76ers. Presently, I'm the general manager for the Orlando Magic, which I co-founded in 1987 and helped lead to the 1995 and 2009 NBA finals.

Because I've personally known so many great team leaders, I understand something about what it takes to build winning teams. My library includes almost 700 books on the subject of leadership, all of which I've read, and a number of which I've written. I've been privileged to address thousands of executives on the subject of leadership, in organizations ranging from Fortune 500 companies and national associations to universities and non-profits.

Developing a winning team requires much more than assembling a group of talented individuals. In my experience, leaders who exhibit the traits of leadership excellence are a prerequisite for all winning teams. In my book *Leadership Excellence*, I identify seven of these traits. They include vision, communication, people skills, competence, boldness, and a serving heart. And the one trait that is absolutely essential is character.

That's why I'm so excited about this excellent book by Lisa Huetteman. She believes, as I do, that core values built on a foundation of character are crucial to the success of any team.

That's true in business, government, sports, and every other field of endeavor.

You may be wondering, if core values are so critical for success, why don't more books on leadership call attention to their importance? May I suggest two possible reasons.

First, our society these days seems to devote much less attention to the subject of character than it did in years past. That's a shame, and it may be one of the reasons why we are experiencing so many unfortunate lapses of integrity in business, government, sports, and other arenas. Lisa performs a valuable service by writing a book that helps overcome this deficiency.

I suspect the second reason why core values are undervalued in our society is because leaders do not understand how to incorporate them in meaningful ways into their daily operations. Core values are given lip service, but they are not taken seriously. Lisa helps rectify this situation, too, by explaining in very practical terms how core values can play a vital role, indeed an indispensable role, in the life of any organization on a day-by-day, decision-by-decision basis.

In the Orlando Magic organization, we deliberately recruit and develop people who will reflect the character we want as a part of our team. We structure good leadership principles into the fabric or our organization, and we expect our people to build on and model the traits we have established. I believe that's one of the major reasons why our franchise has been in the playoffs more than half of the years of its existence (fourteen playoff appearances in twenty-three years).

But overall success is not gauged simply by wins and losses. True success is also measured by key intangibles, such as the response of our fans. Our goal is to serve them, and I am greatly encouraged when adults write to tell me how our players have been positive role models for their kids. I get lots of those letters, and their value to me and our organization is beyond measure. No record book or financial statement is more important to us.

In *The Value of Core Values*, Lisa has done an outstanding job of identifying the principles that make core values valuable. And she supports her exposition with engaging, real-life stories of organizations that have successfully benefited from them. She explains in practical terms how a commitment to core values can promote the success of any team, and she points out the rewards that result from living them every day.

I urge you to read and apply the five keys to values-centered leadership that Lisa highlights in her fine book. If you do, I am convinced that you, too, will appreciate and benefit from the priceless value of core values.

~ Pat Williams
Senior Vice President of the NBA's Orlando Magic
Author of *Leadership Excellence: The Seven Sides of Leadership for the 21st Century*

Preface

L iving by core values promotes organizational success. This I know from my experience in the corporate world, as well as from my years as an organizational consultant. Yet, most companies give core values no more than lip service, if they give them any attention at all. Why is that?

Perhaps it's because many business executives have the mistaken notion that core values and profitability are mutually exclusive. Yes, they know from the daily newspapers how failing to live by core values can lead to a company's downfall. They might even have witnessed such disasters firsthand, as I have. But unfortunately, they don't know about companies where values-centered leadership has been good for business.

So I set out to find organizations that take core values seriously, not just in theory, but in day-to-day practice. I had a hunch that I would discover some that were not only living their core values, but were thriving because of them. And I was right!

The leaders I interviewed turned out to be as inspirational as their stories. I was struck by their positive attitudes and sincere humility. They understand that their personal values set the tone for the entire organization. Like the rest of us, these leaders face daily struggles, but they remain committed to living their core values every day, both individually and organizationally. They hold themselves accountable to the values they espouse to others.

As I conducted my research, I looked for common themes and practices that these companies share. I was able to identify five values-centered leadership principles that I present in this book. If you put these principles into practice, I believe you also will reap the marvelous benefits of living your core values.

In the process of writing this book, I also discovered something else that I didn't expect. I realized that I wasn't consistently living the core values in our business. Occasionally, I was failing to apply the principles that I now advocate in this book.

Writing *The Value of Core Values* prompted me to reassess how I make decisions in my business every day. I hope reading it will do the same for you. My desire is that you'll find the stories encouraging, the questions challenging, the tools practical, and the information valuable. Most of all, I hope you'll realize and appreciate, to a greater degree than ever before, the priceless value of core values.

The Core Value Crisis

"Every young man would do well to remember that all successful business stands on the foundation of morality."
~ Henry Ward Beecher

Chapter 1 – The Core Values Crisis

"Greed, for lack of a better word, is good." So said Gordon Gekko, the infamous character in the 1987 movie *Wall Street*. As we look back over the past few decades, it is interesting to note how fact can mirror fiction. We do in fact have a values crisis in our country. From reading the newspaper or watching the TV news, you and I know all too well what happens to real-life executives who sell themselves out for corporate profits or personal gain. In recent years, a lengthy parade of shipwrecked careers and discredited companies has marched before our eyes.

These "sensational" stories are just the tip of the iceberg. Every day thousands upon thousands of other companies are suffering from expensive, time-consuming, and energy-draining problems with customers, employees, subcontractors and vendors because they either haven't defined core values or they try to take shortcuts around them. This may not always get them in trouble with the law, but the costs are nonetheless significant.

What prompts so many executives to get off course, causing their companies to self-destruct before our eyes? No doubt the answers are complex, but I suspect that one root cause is a lack of adherence to positive core values. In my own experience, I haven't encountered any "sensational" stories that have made the national news, but I have seen plenty of serious business struggles that have one thing in common. They were caused by—or at least exacerbated by—the failure to have and live by organizational core values.

I'll illustrate by sharing three typical examples drawn from my experience. The names and details have been changed to protect confidentiality, but the essential facts are accurate.

3

A family-owned business

"Help me transfer the operations of this business to my children," Steve, the head of a family-owned business said to me in our first meeting. "I want to turn over day-to-day operations so I can retire and pursue other interests."

On the surface, this appeared to be a typical consulting assignment, but it turned out to be "mission impossible." It didn't take me long to see that Steve's personal desires and those of his children were totally out of alignment with the needs of the organization.

None of the family members liked working in the business. They were only there to get their paychecks so they could feed their lifestyles. Some of them routinely came in late, if they came in at all. When they were there, they pretty much did whatever they wanted. In spite of their sloppy work ethic, each sibling felt they were doing more than the next, polluting the workplace with incessant bickering.

For several weeks I struggled to work with Steve and his "leadership team" to discern a common vision and shared values. Unfortunately, values that would benefit both the organization and the individual family members—such as integrity, service, trust, teamwork, or quality—didn't get much traction. At one point Steve blurted out in frustration, "We have no values!"

Actually, Steve and his leadership team did value one thing: profitability. Not organizational profitability, but personal profitability. They all had dreams of a big payday when they could sell the business at a huge profit and each share in the inheritance. Meanwhile, their selfish attitudes and dysfunctional behaviors were damaging the morale of the entire organization, resulting in high employee turnover, poor product quality, and less-than-stellar financial performance.

A non-profit organization

Al, a board member of a non-profit agency, called me in after he had received several complaints from employees about problems in the organization. "Employees are frustrated with the working conditions at our agency," he told me. "Arguments are erupting all over the place, and key people aren't even speaking to each other."

As is the case with most non-profits, Al and his board had done a reasonably good job of defining the mission, strategic objectives, and goals of the organization. The employees generally understood and agreed with them. In fact, most of the staff were attracted to the organization because they were passionate about its mission.

But there was a huge void in the strategic plan. It contained no shared values to shape the culture of the organization, influence hiring, and guide behaviors. People were held accountable for what they did, but not for how they did it.

Consequently, instead of open communication and mutual support, the culture was characterized by gossip and manipulation. Instead of teamwork, people and departments engaged in cut-throat competition. The employees cared more about the mission of the organization—the "cause"—than about their co-workers. Morale and productivity had hit rock bottom. High turnover was severely impacting organizational stability.

A professional services business

"We need help developing a strategic plan to get our firm back on track," Joan, the president of a professional services firm, informed me. "For the first time in years our annual bonus is in jeopardy."

As I conducted my discovery, it became evident that the divisive behaviors of a couple of employees were infecting the rest of the staff like a cancer. The organization's bottom line was suffering.

Joan was already aware of the problem. When I asked her why she hadn't taken action, she replied, "I've spoken to these two people, but my hands are tied. I can't take disciplinary action because they haven't done anything illegal, and they're achieving their stated productivity goals."

Then I asked Joan about the firm's core values. "We don't have any," she replied.

"Your lack of core values makes it difficult for you to address these behavioral issues," I told her. "Because you focus solely on productivity goals without defining acceptable behaviors, you aren't able to hold people accountable. Unless you establish core values and expect people to honor them, morale will continue to decline, taking your firm's profits with it."

Values provide the fundamental framework for success

The organizational struggles I've just related are not unusual. Extrapolating from my sphere of experience, I can only imagine how many individuals and organizations across our country are underachieving because they don't truly appreciate the value of core values. It is difficult to make good decisions about hiring, discipline, marketing, and other operational matters without core values to direct you. Shared core values provide guidelines for productivity and benchmarks for accountability. When values are absent, problems fill the void.

Core values should not be viewed merely as tools for the accomplishment of organizational goals, but rather as seeds for the cultivation of organizational culture. When properly planted and nurtured, core values produce an organizational culture that promotes sustained growth and long-term success.

Core values provide the priorities for creating vision, the principles for developing plans, the guidelines for making decisions, the standards for governing behaviors, and the benchmarks for establishing accountability. Organizations that live by their core values attract high-caliber employees and loyal customers. They are great places to work, and they achieve sustainable profitability.

Core values are a two-way street

On countless occasions, I've met executives who struggle with a lack of fit between their values and the values of the organization. Often, in an effort to meet the expectations of management, they find themselves making substantial compromises in significant areas of their lives.

Susan, one executive I've worked with, had a stressful job with long hours, high profitability goals, strict professional standards, exhausting administrative burdens, and interpersonal communication challenges. Her extreme desire to succeed professionally was intensified by the pressures she felt as the primary "bread winner" for her family.

Shortly after she was promoted into a new leadership role, a large national organization acquired her company and the culture became more political. Because her personal values and the values of the new organization were out of alignment, Susan's health and family life began to suffer. But to impress her new superiors and satisfy her own need to excel, she worked longer and longer hours. That added to her stress, which in turn diminished her productivity.

Both the individual and the organization lose when values

7

are misaligned. But too often no one calls a halt to the downward spiral. Both sides work harder and harder to force a square peg into a round hole.

The simple answer

If the solution to all of these personal and organizational challenges is to begin living in accordance with core values, why don't individuals and companies just do it? I believe one reason is an excessive emphasis on short-term profitability. People and organizations will compromise a great deal—sometimes a great deal too much—to gain financial rewards.

Ignorance and fear are two more possible reasons why companies and individuals give short shrift to core values. They're ill-informed of the substantial benefits of honoring core values and they're afraid it will hurt profitability or the other measures that influence their paychecks.

That's why I've written this book. I want to dispel the false notion that living core values undermines profitable growth. In these pages I share the stories of several leaders who have made the investment in owning, defining, sharing, supporting, and honoring core values. You will learn how they have substantially benefited financially and in other ways. I hope that you'll be encouraged by their successes, so that you also are inspired to benefit from the value of core values.

~ *Questions for Reflection* ~

- Are financial implications the primary consideration that guides your decision making?

- Do you get frustrated with the amount of interpersonal conflict at work? Do you wish that everyone would just learn to get along?

- Do you have a difficult time attracting and retaining good employees?

Are you satisfied with your responses to these questions? If not, the following chapters will illustrate successful models for implementing solutions to the problems you may be experiencing.

Culture, Strategy and Values

"Try not to become a man of success, but rather try to become a man of value."

~ *Albert Einstein*

Chapter 2 – Culture, Strategy and Values

What is more important for business success: an organization's strategy or its culture? That question was posed by a member of an online discussion group of experienced executives, consultants, and coaches. The responses were insightful:

"Strategy is critical," said one, "but without the right culture, change won't happen. Without true commitment, nothing gets accomplished."

"Culture trumps strategy," another agreed. "If there is a radical change in strategy without a corresponding change in culture, that strategy will not succeed."

"Ultimately the right strategy is needed to compete, while the right culture is needed to succeed," added another participant.

"Culture is more important," commented a fourth member of the group. "Belief determines behavior, behavior determines results, and culture strongly influences both. If an elegant strategy runs up against a culture (the norms, beliefs, and behaviors of the employees) that can't or won't support it, that strategy is finished."

I wholeheartedly agree with these responses. An organization's culture—the sum total of its values, attitudes, beliefs, and behaviors—profoundly affects all of its activities and achievements. Organizations whose cultures prize excellence will tend to achieve excellence. Organizations with strong "can-do" attitudes will tend to set and achieve ambitious goals. On the other hand, organizational cultures devoid of positive values are almost certainly destined for mediocrity, or worse.

Growing a winning culture

I like having a nice garden. But frankly, I don't enjoy doing the necessary work. I wish that beautiful flowers would spring up spontaneously. But if I use the "stand-back-and-watch" approach, I know what will happen. No matter how fertile the ground, I'll simply get weeds. In order to have flowers, I have to plant flowers. And what's more, I have to keep watering, weeding, and fertilizing the garden so they'll grow.

Companies are like that. Healthy, productive organizational cultures don't just happen. They need to be cultivated. The culture of an organization is determined primarily by its core values. Organizations, like individuals, become what they value, respect, and believe.

Although I believe that honesty and integrity are fundamental values without which no others can subsist, I am not suggesting that there's one set of core values that's right for every organization, any more than there's one right plant for every type of soil. Some plants, like azaleas, grow best in acidic soil. Others, like cacti, prefer sand. Just as the flowers, soil, lighting and moisture must be compatible for a garden to flourish, the vision, values, culture, and strategy must be in harmony for an organization to succeed.

The most successful organizations deliberately cultivate winning cultures. They consciously choose to live by core values that promote successful attitudes and behaviors. Sowing and nurturing positive core values is an integral component of their organizational strategy.

Unfortunately, many organizations approach core values the way I approach gardening. I know I should take the time to determine the best soil, lighting, moisture, and nutrients for the types of plants I'd like to grow. I know that if I select the wrong plants for my garden—or if I don't take the time to till, fertilize, and cultivate the soil—I won't get the desired results. But proper gardening requires time, which for me is in short supply. So I select flowers that look good in the nursery and hope they will grow where I plant them. A few months later, I usually end up replanting. Not very productive, I know, but I bet I'm not alone.

Many companies operate the same way. They rush their leadership team off to a strategic planning retreat where they identify a few core values they think would be good for their organization. Then they hurry back, "plant" those values, and hope they'll take root. But simply posting your core values on a wall in hopes that people will live them doesn't work. When organizational culture and core values are not integral components of your overall strategy, the results are always disappointing. That's why many organizations have given up on core values altogether.

Abandoning ship

"Giving up" takes two forms. The first is *unconscious* abdication. The leaders think that because they've defined the values, their job is done. They believe that because they've dictated the organization's core values, people will follow.

The second version of "giving up" is *conscious* abdication. It can take two forms. The first occurs when an organization, after making a half-hearted commitment to core values, gives up because the immediate results don't measure up to expectations. Rather than continuing through with commitment, they rationalize failure by saying something like, "We've tried defining core values and it didn't work for us."

The second form of *conscious* abdication occurs when organizations decide in advance that core values are not important. "Identifying core values is fine for big corporations," they say,

15

"but we don't want to lose our informal, small-company culture. Besides, we need to focus on results."

These attitudes reveal a complete misunderstanding of what core values are, as well as an erroneous fear that honoring them will slow growth and hurt profitability. Such misperceptions unfortunately keep many organizations from realizing the benefits.

The fake-plants syndrome

Inside my house I have silk plants. They suit my busy lifestyle because they don't need water, food, or sunlight. But they do have one significant drawback: they don't grow. Yes, they get the job done in a manner of speaking. But if I had more time and energy, I'd much prefer real, vibrant plants over these lifeless imitations.

Companies without core values are like artificial plants: They don't grow. Eventually, the "weeds" of poor morale, high turnover, declining sales, and reduced profits take over and kill the business. It is true that creating a culture founded on core values requires effort. But the benefits are worth the investment. A values-centered culture is the soil in which individuals and organizations can grow and flourish.

CEOs who value core values lead profitable companies that are great places to work. I know this to be true because I've seen it proven in actual situations time and again. Their stories don't make headlines, but they are sensational nonetheless.

~ Questions for Reflection ~

- How would you define your company's culture?
- Is it what you want it to be?
- Do the majority of the people in your organization really enjoy coming to work every day?

If you're not satisfied with your responses to these questions, read on. In the next chapter I'll share how values-based decisions drive a company's continued success.

What Are Core Values?

"Don't judge each day by the harvest you reap but by the seeds that you plant."

~ *Robert Louis Stevenson*

Chapter 3 – What Are Core Values?

Core means *center, heart, nucleus, interior, foundation, mainstay, focal point,* and *substance.*
Values are *principles, standards, morals, ethics,* and *ideals.* Values always have worth, importance, and significance.

It follows then, that core values are the ideals and principles that lie at the very heart of an organization and guide all of its behaviors. They are the foundation upon which all strategies, processes, decisions, and actions rest.

- **Strategies** describe *what* the organization is going to do.
- **Core values** define *how* the organization is going to do it.

A company without a strategy is like a sailboat without a rudder. It will drift without direction or purpose. A company without core values is like a sailboat without a keel. It will capsize!

All organizations have cultures comprised of the underlying beliefs, values, attitudes, and behaviors that determine their performance. Some of these cultures exist by design; others exist simply by default. Successful leaders don't leave their company's culture to chance. They identify and define core values that are aligned with the vision of the business. Then they incorporate the core values they value into the life of the organization on an on-going basis.

The rungs on the ladder

Whether they explicitly recognize it or not, all businesses refer to standards for decision making. These standards are hierarchical, like rungs on a ladder. In some organizations, decisions are made from the bottom rung of the ladder. Leaders of these companies ask, "Is it legal?" The guiding question for companies that operate on the next higher rung is, "Is it ethical?" And from the top rung of the ladder, where values-based companies operate, the primary question is, "Does it honor our core values?" The view is always best from the top.

Mark Mazur practices values-centered leadership. The burly president of MJM Electric, a family-owned and operated commercial electrical contractor, shared how his company makes decisions in light of its values.

> *We wire phosphate mines, breweries, powerhouses, and even nuclear power plants. It's some of the most difficult and dangerous electrical work there is, so safety and quality are our priorities.*
>
> *About three years ago, we had a situation where our workers kept getting multiple finger lacerations on a particular project, so our safety committee recommended giving every employee a pair of cut-proof gloves. They're much better than leather gloves—even a knife won't cut through them—but they cost about ten times as much. There's no law requiring safety gloves.*
>
> *Hard hats are required by law on a job site, but not gloves. But I felt it was the right thing to do, so I gave my OK.*
>
> *The workers liked the new gloves so much they started using them all the time, even at home. They were wearing them out and losing them so fast that it was costing the company a lot of money.*
>
> *So the question came up, how many pairs of these cut-proof gloves should the company provide each employee?*

We decided to give our people as many pairs as they needed and not worry about whether they wore them out, lost them, or took them home. We figured that if we spent $20,000 a year on gloves and nobody cuts a finger it would be money well spent. When our people are happy and trust everything we do, they produce higher quality work. It's that simple.

If MJM had been operating from the bottom rung of the ladder, management wouldn't have furnished gloves at all because they weren't legally required to. If they had been operating from the middle rung, where ethics guide decisions, they might have supplied one pair of gloves. But because the company operates from the highest rung, where core values guide decision making, they supplied as many pairs as necessary.

As a result, MJM attracts the best electrical workers from the unionized labor pool, and it recently was named Small Business of the Year by the Tampa Chamber of Commerce. I believe Mark Mazur's focus on values is a major reason—perhaps the major reason—for the company's remarkable success.

The slippery slope

All too often organizations that descend the ladder from core values to ethics to legality are on a slippery slope to problems. Some companies even drop below the bottom rung, so that "Is it legal?" gradually becomes "Will we get caught?" When that happens, serious trouble is around the corner.

Under the pressures of day-to-day business, it's amazing—and somewhat frightening—to see how rapidly almost any behavior can be justified. Deviations from core values usually begin with rationalizations based on circumstances.

Consider this example, which is a paraphrase of an actual situation:

Bill is the owner of a computer systems integration firm that gets most of its business by responding to requests for proposals (RFP). In its responses, Bill's company typically must affirm that the company's bid complies with the specifications set forth in the RFP. One day, while reviewing a proposal prior to submission, he noticed that the engineer had failed to check the box indicating compliance.

"The RFP specified outdated items," explained the engineer. "I based our bid on state-of-the-art techniques that will give the customer a much better product, while putting us in a good position to be low bidder. It's the win-win proposition. But that's why I can't in good conscience check the box affirming that our proposal complies with the specs of the RFP."

Bill knew that if they didn't check the box, their proposal would almost certainly be eliminated from consideration. That put him in a quandary. If he told the engineer to check the box anyway, he would essentially be asking the engineer to lie. That would certainly violate his values, as well as the company's. On the other hand, if Bill submitted a proposal that conformed to the specs, it would increase the cost substantially and his company would probably lose the job. As a result, he might have to let some employees go.

The people in your organization face problems like Bill's every day, and they look to you for clarity and guidance about how to make decisions and solve them. If you compromise on values and allow or encourage others to do the same, what kind of example are you setting? If honoring core values becomes a function of circumstances, you'll find yourself at the edge of a slippery slope. Minor infractions that can be easily justified—such as indicating your bid complies with the specifications in an RFP when it does not—soon grow into more major violations. Situational leadership with regard to honoring core values will cause people to lose respect for you and the organization, and they will be confused about what is an acceptable way to think, act, and make decisions.

Because values underlie our attitudes, behaviors, and decisions every minute of every day, whether we realize it or not, it's vital for organizations to intentionally define and communicate the core values they want to guide behavior.

Is profitability a core value?

Profitability is a laudable business goal. Without profits, a company cannot continue to serve its customers, employ its people, reward its investors, and contribute to its community. I'm all for profits. But defining profitability as a core value can lead to problems. When a company faces difficult decisions that impact profits, the core value of profitability will trump other core values virtually every time. Pursuing short-term profitability at the expense of other core values hurts long-term profitability.

Robert H. Schuller is attributed with saying "Anyone can count the seeds in an apple, but only God can count the number of apples in a seed." Core values are the seeds from which the culture of an organization grows. When positive values are planted and nurtured, they develop into positive attitudes and behaviors that yield profitable results. But that doesn't happen overnight. To appreciate the value of core values, you must look beyond the immediate to the ultimate, beyond the visible to the potential. Just as the fruit produced by one apple seed can be unlimited, the true value of core values is immeasurable.

~ Questions for Reflection ~

- Do short-term results trump long-term impact in your decision-making process?

- How do you determine the course of action when the short-term and long-term implications of a decision conflict?

- Are your core values an integral part of your decision-making criteria?

As you answer the above questions, consider how your current approach is working for you. If you're looking for improved results, find out what other companies have done to achieve consistent long-term success. In the next chapter, I'll lay out the five keys to organizational success through values-centered leadership.

The Five Keys

"Wise are those who learn that the bottom line doesn't always have to be their top priority."

~ *William Arthur Ward*

Chapter 4 – The Five Keys

L ater in this book you'll meet numerous business leaders whose companies successfully operate in accordance with shared core values. I think you'll be impressed by their humility, courage, and commitment. None would say that living by core values is easy. They readily acknowledge that while adherence to values simplifies decision making and produces significant long-term benefits, it frequently requires short-term sacrifices. Nevertheless, not one of these leaders could imagine doing business any other way.

These organizations are from diverse industries, and they're led by people with vastly different personalities. But they all have one thing in common: they've been successful because they've lived core values. They recognize that leaders drive values, values drive behaviors, and behaviors drive performance.

Keys to success

How have these businesses been able to reap the benefits of living core values while so many others have failed? What are the keys to their success? Can we discern any general principles that have guided their actions? Yes, I believe we can. I submit that the following five principles are the keys to achieving organizational success through values-centered leadership:

1. **Owning your values**: Your personal and organizational values should be an expression of who you are at your core. If you're not committed to them, no one else will be.
2. **Defining core values**: You must give meaning to your chosen values by creating clear definitions so everyone concerned understands what behaviors they advocate and forbid.

3. **Sharing core values**: You need to communicate your core values constantly and consistently so that everyone in the organization understands and owns them.
4. **Institutionalizing core values**: You must weave your values into the fabric of your organization so they influence all actions and decisions.
5. **Honoring core values**: You must regard your company's core values as non-negotiable or they will become inconsequential.

Note in the diagram below how living core values is a self-reinforcing process. Coming full circle, honoring values always increases ownership.

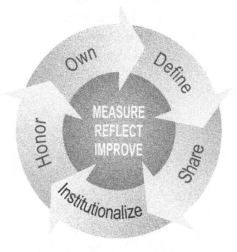

Florida Hospital – Putting Principles into Practice

To illustrate the five keys, I'll describe how Florida Hospital puts each of these principles into practice:

Owning Your Values

Florida Hospital in Orlando is part of a nationwide healthcare system founded in 1866 by Seventh-day Adventists. The hospital system's vision is to care for the mind and spirit as well as for the body. Over the years its mission has remained the same: To extend the healing ministry of Christ. From the beginning, the pioneers of this organization, guided by founding members James and Ellen White, remained true to their own values. Defying the "truths" of the day and holding strong to their values, they boldly challenged common assumptions about health and hygiene and founded an organization that was radically counter-cultural.

In the middle of the 1800s, doctors believed smoking was good for the lungs, fresh night air was harmful, diets high in sugar and fat were healthy, bathing and sunlight were hazardous, and draining blood was an effective cure for many illnesses. In founding their health care facility, the Whites took a novel approach which emphasized the natural remedies of fresh air, sunshine, exercise, rest, pure water, good nutrition, and a spiritual connection.

In 1908, the Adventists opened their first facility in Florida—a simple farmhouse with twenty patient beds and one physician—that later became known as Florida Hospital. Today, Florida Hospital has more than 4,000 physicians treating upwards of two million patients per year at 22 hospital locations and 21 urgent care facilities throughout Florida, and it's still growing. The medical pioneers of this organization were true to their own values and beliefs in founding a system of care that defied the

31

"truths" of the day and created an organization that treats the whole person—body, mind, and spirit.

Owning your values often requires taking risks and departing from the norm. That demands courage, confidence, and commitment. These are the qualities displayed by the early leaders at Florida Hospital and by the other leaders highlighted in this book.

 Defining Core Values

In developing their healthcare organizations, the early Adventist leaders looked to the life of Christ for inspiration. From their study of Scripture, the Adventists realized that Jesus devoted a great deal of His time on earth healing the sick and helping those in need. They wanted to pattern their healthcare services after His ministry.

More recently, as hospital leadership defined the organization's values, they looked to the Bible's account of creation to discern what God had in mind for whole-person wellness. In an effort to create a healthy work environment and improve the well-being of those who turn to them for care, Florida Hospital followed these eight CREATION principles:

{ Provide the right information at the right time so informed decisions can be made to meet our patients' needs } **C**HOICE

{ Ensure balance between the stresses of delivering modern medicine and the quality of the workforce needed to provide superior care } **R**EST

{ We are affected as much by what lies outside of us as we are by what is occurring inside of us } **E**NVIRONMENT

{ Being active promotes good health and a sharp mind } **A**CTIVITY

{ Trust in God – Florida Hospital recognizes the importance of the spiritual dimension of healing } **T**RUST

{ The effectiveness of the team is greater than the sum of its parts. Loneliness is a primary contributor to chronic disease } **I**NTERPERSONAL RELATIONSHIPS

{ Maintaining hope and having a can-do attitude will contribute to superior outcomes } **O**UTLOOK

{ A good diet will result in a sharp mind and improve health } **N**UTRITION

Florida Hospital's core values—integrity, compassion, balance, excellence, stewardship, and teamwork—flow directly from these CREATION principles and the organization's mission and vision. The hospital's leadership understands that individual words, such as integrity or excellence, can mean different things to different people. To have value, core values must be described in behavioral terms within the context of the organization's mission and vision. Therefore, in 2007 a team of senior leaders, physicians, directors/managers, frontline staff members, and patients reaffirmed and expanded Florida Hospital's core values to include the following specific definitions and expected behavioral standards:

Core Value	INTEGRITY
Definition	When one's words and actions create trust, as evidenced by being truthful, respectful and consistent
Behavior	▪ *Consistently acts in the best interest of our patients, family members, co-workers and the hospital*
	▪ *Speaks up when something appears wrong or inappropriate*
	▪ *Accepts responsibility for one's actions and the resulting outcomes*
	▪ *Follows through with one's commitments*
	▪ *Is consistently transparent, open and honest in one's dealings with others*

Core Value	**COMPASSION**
Definition	Meeting individual needs with kindness, care and empathy
Behavior	▪ *Anticipates and responds quickly to the needs of others using SHARE principles*
	▪ *Acknowledges others by name and greets people with a smile and direct eye contact*
	▪ *Treats others with respect and dignity*
	▪ *Actively listens to understand the needs of others*
	▪ *Ensures care and comfort by attending to the basic needs of patients, family members, and co-workers every day*

Core Value	**BALANCE**
Definition	Harmony in one's professional, personal and community life, as well as in one's own body, mind and spirit.
Behavior	▪ *Embraces the CREATION model and encourages others to do the same*
	▪ *Demonstrates a passion for continuous learning*
	▪ *Promotes healing through a sense of humor, touch and prayer*
	▪ *Contributes to the morale of co-workers through a continual focus on both clinical and operational results*

Core Value	**EXCELLENCE**
Definition	Provides care and services that are safe, reliable and patient-centered, driving extraordinary clinical, operational and financial performance
Behavior	▪ *Creates a patient experience which is consistently reliable and safe*
	▪ *Exceeds performance expectations in all five elements of Exceeding Excellence*
	▪ *Consistently follows institutional and regulatory guidelines, putting safety first every time*
	▪ *Advocates for the patient and, where necessary, breaks down barriers to exceptional care*
	▪ *Holds self and others accountable for results*

Core Value	**TEAMWORK**
Definition	An environment that values diversity of thought and background, while encouraging individuals to share their different perspectives
Behavior	▪ *Shares credit with others on the team*
	▪ *Encourages a strong, inclusive team spirit through positive feedback, recognition of others and celebrating success*
	▪ *Consistently includes others affected by a decision in the decision making*
	▪ *Ensures the success of the team by sharing all relevant information*
	▪ *Seeks to retain the best talent to assure team strength*

Core Value	**STEWARDSHIP**
Definition	Ensures sustainability and pre-eminence in patient care by responsively managing resources entrusted to us
Behavior	▪ *Thinks like an owner by adding value each day to protect and sustain the brand*
	▪ *Efficiently utilizes the tools and resources provided to enhance the business*
	▪ *Understands Florida Hospital's business and the importance of individual contributions to our overall success*
	▪ *Considers long-term versus short-term business results of each action taken*
	▪ *Consistently strives to eliminate unnecessary costs for Florida Hospital*

Florida Hospital recognizes the importance of well-defined core values. Vaguely defined values provide no guidance or accountability. They simply cause confusion, apathy, and frustration.

Sharing Core Values

Florida Hospital's leaders promote the organization's values first and foremost by living them. Since the organization's core values are based on the teachings of Christ and His healing ministry, all senior leaders dedicate themselves to this higher purpose. At every new employee orientation, a senior leader talks about the importance of Florida Hospital's mission, vision, and values. Leaders open meetings and forums with a devotional message and prayer.

The hospital also employs multiple, overlapping channels to communicate and promote its mission, vision, and values to staff, physicians, patients, volunteers, partners, suppliers and community citizens. As shown by the table on the next page, sharing is systematic and comprehensive.

To enhance the effectiveness of structured communications, hospital leadership "formalizes informal communications." They deliberately and consistently promote the organization's vision, mission, and core values by spending time where physicians and staff congregate. In both structured evaluations and informal conversations, they consistently ask for feedback from employees and others about how the organization can better live in accordance with its mission and values.

Florida Hospital devotes at least as much attention and commitment to sharing its core values as it gives to any of its other important marketing initiatives, and it uses the same methodical steps: design, implementation, measurement, and improvement. It invests significant resources to ensure that its values are communicated, understood, and lived.

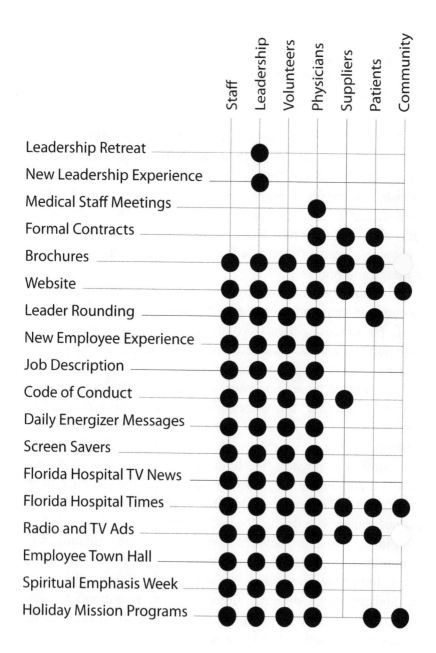

Institutionalizing Core Values

To have a positive impact day after day, year after year, core values must be woven into the fabric of the organization. They must be institutionalized.

On their first day of work, new Florida Hospital employees receive a four-hour introduction to the hospital's legacy, mission, vision, and values. They sign a Code of Conduct, which is renewed annually, promising to comply with expected behaviors.

Annual performance reviews evaluate employee performance against these standards, and a developmental plan is created for each employee that stresses the alignment of individual and organizational goals. Two-way evaluations are built into the review process. These "upward and downward" evaluations are a radical departure from standard business practice. In most organizations, annual reviews are one-way, top-down conversations.

After their first thirty days of employment, employees participate in a second orientation where they are asked if the organization practices what it preaches with respect to core values. During their annual performance reviews, employees are invited to evaluate the organization and suggest improvements.

All members of the workforce are encouraged to report illegal or unethical behaviors 24/7/365 using CompassPoint, a compliance hotline. Florida Hospital also has institutionalized external and internal evaluations of its performance, in the same way that many companies use internal and external auditors to evaluate their financial practices.

When I recently walked through the halls of Florida Hospital's

Orlando campus, the organization's mission and values are physically evident everywhere, from the design and layout of the physical building to the artwork displayed on the walls. In a large meeting room I observed an employee-staffed exhibition that promoted teamwork, balance, and excellence. Across the hall, a town hall meeting was taking place. Although it was relaxed and conversational, this was not a random, informal gathering. It was a thoughtfully designed process for communicating core values and soliciting ideas to improve patient care.

In support of the value of compassion, boxes of food items were stacked and ready for shipment to families in need. They had been prepared by participants in the hospital's Spiritual Ambassadors Initiative, a formalized program designed to bring spirituality into the workplace through mission projects that honor the values of generous stewardship and unselfish teamwork.

Florida Hospital's budgeting processes are aligned with its priorities. Consistent with the value of excellence, the hospital recently invested $60 million in new software that promises to improve patient safety by reducing potential problems associated with the interactions of different medications.

To be effective, core values must be institutionalized. Institutionalizing core values doesn't require bureaucracy, but it does demand creativity and intentionality. At Florida Hospital, core values are integrated into its structure, processes, policies, and procedures in a way that supports living them every day.

Honoring Core Values

Florida Hospital's mission statement and core values are more than mere words. They are the non-negotiable standards for guiding and measuring every action, decision, and expenditure. Everyone associated with the organization is held accountable to them. Management knows that without accountability, human nature is prone to either deny that problems exist (conscious abdication) or to simply hope they don't exist (unconscious abdication). Florida Hospital has integrated internal and external evaluations into its operations to ensure that its core values are honored.

Every other year, the hospital invites senior leaders from other hospitals within the Florida Hospital system to visit a facility and conduct an internal peer review. The evaluation team meets with staff members at all levels and makes recommendations about how the hospital can more effectively live its mission, vision, and values. On alternate years, an external review is conducted by senior leaders from Adventist Health System (AHS) hospitals outside the Florida Hospital System. The evaluation team also includes community leaders and other stakeholders. The feedback and recommendations from these internal and external reviews are incorporated into budgeted action plans.

Florida Hospital honors its core values, even when that requires turning down potentially lucrative opportunities or risking financial loss. In recent years, it has bypassed growth opportunities totaling nearly $1 billion because they threatened to dilute the mission.

41

In 2008, the hospital was confronted with a significant values-related decision while constructing a new building on its Orlando campus. To lay the building's foundation, trucks would have to pour cement continuously for approximately twenty-five hours. This would have to be completed during a weekend because the large caravan of trucks required to transport the cement would clog Orlando's busy highway system during the week.

From a strictly business standpoint, the best plan would be to start pouring on Saturday so as to allow plenty of time to complete the job, with some leeway for inclement weather or other delays. Hospital management was informed that not completing the project in one weekend could add approximately $4 million to the cost of the project. But there was one big glitch. Working on Saturday (the Sabbath) would violate a key tenet of faith for Seventh-day Adventists.

After prayerful deliberation, hospital leadership decided to honor the Sabbath and start pouring cement on Sunday. This decision, although weighty, was easy to make because management understood that the long-term cost of not honoring the organization's core values was much greater than the potential loss of $4 million.

At Florida Hospital, all decisions and actions are continually evaluated in light of the organization's mission and values. Core values are consistently honored in all decisions because they're regarded as non-negotiable by all concerned.

~ Questions for Reflection ~

- Is your organization practicing the five keys to organizational success?

- Would I get a consistent response if I randomly asked three of your employees to define your company's core values?

- Would I get favorable responses if I asked how well your company lives its values?

Owning Your Values

"Nothing so conclusively proves a man's ability to lead others as what he does from day to day to lead himself."
~ *Thomas J. Watson*

Chapter 5 – Owning Your Values

W hat do you value? What is really important to you on a personal level? What things would you not want to give up for all the money in the world? What would be important to you if you did have all the money in the world?

Gaining clarity about your personal values is essential to living life with passion and purpose. Clarity about personal values also is important on an organizational level because all organizations are made up of individuals. The degree of success or failure of the organizational unit hinges on whether the values of the individuals are in alignment with those of the organization.

I love variety in my garden. I find it interesting that the mixture of flowers, with their different colors, shapes, and sizes, all depend on the same sunlight and rain for growth and survival.

The same is true for organizations. In order for them to thrive, they need people with a variety of talents, skills and behavioral styles. But to achieve its full potential, this diversity needs to be rooted in shared core values. An organization must own clearly defined core values, and those values must in turn be owned by each individual in the organization. Diversity in talents and personalities is good. Diversity in core values is not.

Core values shape the culture of the organization. Individuals who do not fit the culture will eventually be forced out, either voluntarily or involuntarily. Who is responsible for this cultural fit, the individual or the organization? The answer is both!

All values begin at the individual level

Personal responsibility begins with a commitment to clearly defined values. People who are uncertain about what they value—

what attitudes and behaviors they regard as non-negotiable—are prone to wander from one job to another looking for meaning and purpose. Unfortunately, they don't find the passion and fulfillment they seek because they lack a foundation of core values on which to build. I've experienced this in my own life in the past, and I've observed it in the lives of many of the executives I have coached.

If you work for an organization where you are being asked to compromise your personal values, perhaps it's time for a change. When personal values and organizational values are misaligned, both the individual and the organization suffer.

Organizational responsibility starts with personal commitment

The individuals within the organization must be willing to be held accountable to the organization's core values, and they must be willing to hold others accountable to them.

Leadership needs to be so strongly committed to the organization's core values that they will only hire individuals who share them. They need to feel so strongly that adherence to core values is the most reliable and rewarding path to personal and professional success that they will always support individuals in living them.

You will achieve the greatest professional success when your values are aligned with the core values of the organization for which you work. To find the right fit, you must first own your own values. Then you are in a position to take an objective look at the organization you are (or are considering) working for to determine whether you can buy into its values.

Not many organizations encourage individuals to clarify and own their personal values. Most of the time you must take the initiative, but that doesn't diminish the importance of the process.

What does "owning core values" mean?

On an individual basis, owning core values starts with clarifying what is most important to you. When seeking employment, look for a company that values what you value. Expend the time and energy to find a good fit. Have the courage to stick to your convictions, going against conventional wisdom if necessary. Don't compromise on your personal values when making decisions about your professional life.

Several of the CEOs highlighted in this book started their own companies precisely because their personal values strongly conflicted with the values of the organizations for which they worked. Their individual values motivated and empowered them to found and lead companies with well-developed organizational core values.

The core values of an organization and the values of individuals within the organization may not be identical, but they must always be in alignment. This is especially true of the leaders, but it also applies to every other person in the organization.

Values you can bank on

Roy Hellwege started his career in the leadership training program of a bank that had $3.5 billion in assets. Twenty-three years later it had assets of $117 billion, and he was president of their Tampa Bay/St. Petersburg operations. It was a great situation and he planned to stay there until retirement. But then some things happened that took Roy's career in a different direction. Here's his story:

I was troubled by the way the bank had changed. To compete with the larger banks, we started centralizing everything. We became more bureaucratic and impersonal. So when someone approached me about becoming president of another bank, I accepted.

That was a mistake. It soon became obvious that the values and the moral standards I had grown up with really weren't prevalent in that bank. Management took a lot of shortcuts. Making the deal was everything; people were secondary. Ultimately the CEO and I didn't see eye to eye, so I ended up leaving.

While I was figuring out what to do next, the CEO of another bank asked me to become its president.

I said OK, and for a while that worked out well. The bank was prospering. But only eighteen months into the job, I received a phone call from the audit department informing me that the CEO who had hired me had been terminated by the board of directors for questionable behavior.

That caused me to do some soul searching. What was wrong with my decision-making process that caused me to keep going into these bad situations?

About this time I was invited to join a small group of CEOs who got together monthly to talk about business issues from a Biblical perspective. I'd always thought there should be a separation between church and the workplace, but as I participated in this group, I began to see the need to integrate my personal and professional values.

Roy Hellwege went on to start a new bank founded on the principles and values that he personally owned and honored.

If you are a leader, your example speaks far louder than your words

Suncoast Team Services annually provides more than $33 million of design/build services to business clients. Tom Strickland, the company's president, believes that leaders should boldly live their personal values:

> *Some people, even some who are strong Christians, struggle with faith in the workplace. They say to me, "My faith is what I do on my time. It's not what I do on the company's time." That reminds me of some star athletes who say, "I don't want to be an example." But like it or not, that's what they are.*
>
> *The same is true for those of us who are business leaders and owners. The people who work for us are looking to us to set the example. I don't care if you don't want to be an example; the fact is you are. We have an opportunity and a responsibility. We can help change a lot of things for the better if we step up to the plate.*

Commitment and compromise

It's one thing to "have" values; it's another to "own" them. Ownership entails far more responsibility and commitment than mere possession. In the midst of day-to-day struggles to achieve legitimate business objectives, you'll encounter countless temptations to compromise your values. The most difficult thing about these temptations is that most will present themselves as shades of gray. Lying in the gray area are trade-offs between *common* industry practices and *ethical* business practices— "You have to pay a 'facilitation fee' if you want to do business in that country." Or, more importantly, in the gray area is the trade-off between what is *material* and what is *right*—"I ignored paying the tax because it wasn't material. It would have cost more than what I owed to process the payment."

When I use the term "compromise," I'm not referring just to matters of legality and ethics, although those issues do sometimes arise. Neither am I passing moral judgment on one set of values versus another, although I do believe in certain truths. What I am talking about is having integrity, so that your values truly reflect who you are and who you want to be.

Whether you are a CEO, mid-level manager, or individual contributor, you must be clear about your own values. You need to own your own values before you can effectively commit to the organization's values. And you must commit to the organization's values before you can expect commitment from others.

~ Questions for Reflection ~

- Do you have a written, well-defined set of personal core values?
- Do you tend to justify decisions that violate your values?
- Are your personal values in alignment with the core values of your organization?

ExecuJet Charter Services, Inc.

Peter Cunzolo founded ExecuJet in 1994 with one plane, one business plan, one investor, and a dream: to build a business that puts the customer first, while providing the ultimate first-class flying experience. Today, with seven aircraft and more than twenty employees, ExecuJet provides world-class charter flights twenty-four hours a day, seven days a week, 365 days a year. Mr. Cunzolo is the owner and *CEO.*

Owning Our Values

Early in my career I flew international air ambulances for several companies. They were interesting jobs, but the companies were terrible places to work. Profit was everything; customers and employees were secondary. There wasn't any transparency, nor were you given the whole story. There were no core principles or values. You were simply expected to get your job done, get paid, and move on.

I knew in my heart that there had to be a better way. So I left aviation for a while and began praying, "Father, I know I can do this, and I know I can run a business the way You would want it to be run, where the employees would be respected and the customers would never be mistreated or lied to. But I need Your help. If You help me, I will never treat my customers or employees the way I was treated, and I know I'm going to do the right thing by You."

That was my prayer. It was almost my mantra. I developed a plan and started looking for investors. After a couple of dead ends, I happened to cross paths with a man who helped me launch ExecuJet. And from day one, the company prospered. Five years later, this investor allowed me to completely buy his ownership stake of the business. We had done the deal on a handshake, and he absolutely and totally kept his word.

Defining Our Values

When I started my business, I wanted to go back to basics. That meant treating customers as I would like to be treated. It meant treating employees with kindness and respect and benevolence, and making an effort to enrich their lives.

Our mission statement is "To be the leading aviation service provider through the consistent application of our core values of safety, service, and excellence." I've been in aviation for more than twenty-six years, and I've never felt more secure in an aircraft than I am when I'm in the ones I'm flying right now. This is a credit and testimony to the care, commitment, and loyalty of our team. It indicates the type of culture we have created at ExecuJet.

Sometimes our people lose their focus, particularly during trying economic times. Although they can recite the core values and they understand our mission, sometimes they need reassurance, as we all do. Our three core values provide the focus and the empowerment to act in favor of our customers.

Sharing Our Values

We review our core values with our people on a continual basis. We've put those core values everywhere in print. Attached to the ceiling of our hangar is a huge banner that has our company name and our tag line of "Safety-Service-Excellence."

We have staff meetings and pilot meetings every month to bring people up to speed on new developments in the industry and in the company. We always bring up the core values. We also do this on an individual basis during the month.

Our typical clients are high-net-worth individuals and companies that have sales from $2 million up. These are the people who generally can afford charter. Our employees are our front-line ambassadors. If they do what's right with our customers, our company will appear head and shoulders above the rest. And that's what our people do.

Here's a story that illustrates how they do that. We had a customer who flies frequently on the same aircraft. But one time, due to scheduling constraints, she had to take another plane. Her regular crew, of their own volition and on their day off, came out to the airport to give her a bouquet of flowers just before she departed. Isn't that something!

Now, I wish I could say that I'm the genius behind all of this, but I'm not. I'm surrounded by people who are extremely capable, loyal, dedicated, and caring. They are the reasons for the successes we enjoy.

We get letters, e-mails, and phone calls from our customers— at least one a week—describing what made their flights so special, or what the pilots or the maintenance team did to make sure that they could meet their schedule.

We post those letters and e-mails, and we reward the people involved with gift cards or other things for their families. They're a good sign that our people are living and working day to day according to the company's core values.

Institutionalizing Our Values

Our core values are very closely intertwined with our day-to-day operations. On virtually every business deal and every charter, we have team meetings to make sure that people are always reminded of what we expect and what we want to provide as our product.

It all starts with the hiring process. I hate to say that we hire to fit the mold, because it's really not that. It's more a matter of finding people who share the same goals, vision, passion, and values. When you find people that fit, it goes a lot easier once they're on board.

People we hire come to realize what type of operation we are and how we handle things with customers and employees. It's almost as if the best seek us out and are led to us. From the beginning, we knew what we wanted to do, which is the right thing, and the right ingredients started to fall into place.

Most of our employees have come to us via word of mouth. I think they know they will be respected and treated fairly. That's been the biggest part of the draw. It's had very little to do with money.

We've noticed that the people who stood the test of time always had very good personal qualities: respect, trust, loyalty, and dedication. During the interview, we explicitly talk about our core values.

If job candidates are fidgety or uncomfortable during the interview, that's usually an indication to us that it's not a fit. If they don't have any compelling life experiences to relate—times when they've helped somebody or done something really cool— or if they seem to just want a job, that fact presents itself in their behavior and body language. You can usually tell if there's chemistry or not.

Recently two of the senior managers put together a team-building weekend on their own initiative, without my assistance or input. It was a camping and canoeing weekend that was an absolute blast. It concentrated on our company mission, core values, and team building. This is one of the reasons why this company is so blessed, and that I absolutely believe we have the finest talent available in this industry. This is very descriptive of the type of company culture we have committed to cultivating here at our company.

Honoring Our Values

It's not always easy to live or work by your values. There are times—it happens a lot—when we have to turn down business because the conditions would cause us to contradict our values. Customers may want us to do things that are unsafe or would go beyond our certification and liability limits. For example, we might be asked to take someone who isn't ambulatory. They might tell us they're medically okay, but we know it's really more of air ambulance flight.

Most of our competitors will take those flights without a second thought because they want the cash flow. They'll put oxygen on board and take off. But what happens if something really bad transpires? Have they really behaved responsibly toward that customer? We don't take that kind of business. It's not right for our employees, our company, or our customers.

There is a lot of dishonesty in segments of aviation. Some owners of aircraft hold no aviation certification from the FAA, and they constantly engage in what's called "uncertificated" charter, which is to say that they are operating without the proper charter certifications by the DOT and FAA. One of our biggest challenges is converting those customers who are used to paying very little for those illegal flights into charter customers who will pay market rates.

And then there are other companies who are certificated but whose maintenance is sub-par. I would never put my family in any of their aircraft. I would never fly them. And yet they're flying

59

the general public for drastically reduced rates because the flying public just doesn't know.

We won't take a flight or continue in a contract that is not going to allow us to enrich the lives of our employees and our customers, while staying true to our core values and our company culture. There are some customers who just aren't worth having if they're going to ask you to stray from the standards you're committed to. There's no reward in that.

Sales pressures

We had a customer who hired us as consultants to help him acquire an aircraft. He was so gung-ho to have this aircraft, he wouldn't heed our advice. We tried to tell him it wasn't the right plane for him—it was going to need a lot of work—but he wouldn't listen.

We were even under pressure from the selling agent. He told us he would give us part of his commission as an incentive to do the deal. "Yeah, the aircraft has a big inspection coming up," he admitted, "but it will pass."

We walked away. I don't need the money that badly. I don't want to run into this guy somewhere down the road and hear him say, "You sold me this airplane and it cost me an extra $250,000 just to bring it up to compliance."

It's just not in my constitution to do the kind of deal that would result in that kind of dissatisfaction. It's not what I want my employees ever to do. It's not the example I want to set. Bottom line, it's lying. Yes, we would've earned a great commission to complete that deal, but I would've lost a repeat customer because I wouldn't have done right by him. I would go so far as to say that I had sinned against him.

That customer bought the airplane through somebody else.

He came back several years later and handed us the project again. We had to make a lot of the necessary repairs required at the time of purchase, plus additional repairs his last management company failed to perform.

This gentleman ended up spending a lot more money on maintenance than he should have, and it could have been avoided. We tried to tell him, and he didn't listen. However, at the end of the day we were able to eventually help him at the back end of it. That kind of thing happens all the time, and it has made us the go-to company that can fix these kinds of problems.

Accountability

Our commitment to core values encourages accountability. I would say that all of our people have enough care and concern for their fellow employees that they will do whatever they have to do to help them finish well.

We've got a pilot who is absolutely spectacular. She is a model employee, and she's also somewhat of a mentor. If someone isn't performing, she'll take that person aside and say, "Hey, this is not how we do things here. Here's what we need to do differently. What do you think?"

Other people do that, too. Our director of operations and our director of maintenance are responsible for specific functions, but they absolutely will get involved in day-to-day operations to ensure the success of not just the company, but of the individuals. If anyone has an issue, whether it's personal or professional, they can get that person's ear, and there will be a call to action on behalf of that person.

We have a culture of trust and transparency, where people feel comfortable enough to speak the truth in love. If you don't have a close-knit group of people, you won't be comfortable having discussions of that type. You might find it awkward, or maybe you won't even care enough.

But if you have a group of people who are familiar with one another, and they have backed each other up and have mutual respect, when someone has kind of fallen off the wagon, so to speak, you can pull them aside and say, "This isn't like you. What's going on? How did this happen?" Those conversations become very easy because you're related in a sense.

Speaking the truth in love is hard to do, but it's so valuable. People know that you're not just picking, but that you really care. You care enough and respect them enough to tell them the truth.

I get it too, which is nice because that's accountability for me. If I'm having a low day, my directors will catch me and say, "What's wrong? You aren't yourself today. Anyway we can help? We need you to step up."

When you own the place, you don't have the luxury of having low days. Everybody feeds off of you. If you're down because you've got a cold or something, they're going to think something is wrong with the company. In a sense, you don't get to be human. It's nice to have guys who will pick up on that to make sure that you're straight. We do that for each other.

We're a young company, and we've got several long-term employees who have double-digit years of service with us, and a lot more who have been with us eight or nine years. This is a hard company to get hired on with, but once you're here, you're here to stay.

With some people, no matter how hard you try, you're not going to reach them for whatever reason. Maybe they didn't have the proper values from the beginning. People who don't feel comfortable functioning within the guidelines that we have soon leave the organization.

As the CEO, I constantly need to beat the big bass drum and

say, "Keep your balance. I don't need you here at 7 p.m. You need to be at home with your family. If you think that one last thing you're going to do here is going to make a difference, it's not. If you're home with your family and you're happy, you'll come back tomorrow fresh. That little project that you thought you absolutely had to get done will be here, and you'll get it done effectively and efficiently."

It's not unusual for me to call our director of maintenance and say, "Hey, I'm leaving. Why aren't you? I don't expect you to be here. I expect you to be on your way home."

We have enough care and concern about each other that we will prop each other up. We will try to help someone who has issues. We will try to do whatever we have to do to get them across the goal line. It's that whole finishing-well concept.

The Value of Core Values

I am so blessed because I absolutely have the finest aviation personnel the industry has to offer. If you watch them walk around and look at their body language or see their demeanor, you will notice that no one is long-faced. No one!

Bigger barns aren't better. To have your family and your health and to just have joy, that's really and truly what matters most. To me, that's the success of it—when you go home and you laugh and you have a great evening with your family. Our family is able to have quality time together, even in simply doing nothing in particular but just giggling together and telling stories or playing a game.

It doesn't have anything to do with money. I think that's probably what the message is. How do you find your inner spirit—your inner joy—that God really wants you to have? That's it for me.

I'm a type A. I'm a hard charger about making sure things tick and that we maintain our profitability, and I'm not afraid to make tough decisions. But I do have a sense of calm and peace when it comes to these situations because I know where my strength is coming from. I know who is providing. I know who is protecting me and my employees and their families.

My prayer is, "Please help me be a steward to Your people, to make ExecuJet a safe haven for those You want here." And that's it. The rest is up to Him. I don't have to know everything. I just have to figure out what to do when He gives it to me.

If I didn't have my faith and I didn't have the blessings that I have—my family, my health, the people I've been blessed to work with—nothing else would work. That's got to be it in a nutshell.

This is a very competitive business, but we have maintained our profitability. It's God's providence. In a day and age when people want God to go away, I'm glad to be able to tell this story.

Defining Core Values

"What will become compellingly important is absolute clarity of shared purpose and a set of principles of conduct—sort of institutional genetic code—that every member of the organization understands in a common way, and with deep conviction."

~ *Dee Hock*

Chapter 6 – Defining Core Values

In my work as a consultant and business coach, I often find myself talking to executives about core values. Most tell me their organizations have them and they're very focused on them. But when I ask what they are, the typical response is something like, "They're integrity and service and ... I can't think of the others right now, but we have them."

Other leaders at least are able to name their organization's values. They may even have memorized them. But when I ask what the values mean and how they relate to everyday business matters, I'm met with a blank stare.

To be effective, core values must be clearly defined. That requires dedicated leadership by the CEO, with the collaboration and buy-in of others within the organization.

Collaboration increases commitment. People who share in defining core values are more likely to participate in living them.

Meaningful core values must be integrally aligned with the organization's vision and mission. Just as a cactus will not grow in the Artic, the perfect culture for a high-tech company will almost certainly be a terrible misfit for a law firm. No one set of core values is right for every organization.

When your company's core values support your vision and mission—when they are an essential element of what you want to be and where you want to go—you will consider any departure from them to be unprofitable in the broadest sense of that term. When you view success through the prism of your core values, violating them will become tantamount to failure.

Defining values is a two-step process

First, the foundational principles that will define the organization's relationships with its customers, employees, suppliers, partners, and other stakeholders must be identified. These principles are the core values. It is imperative that they are aligned with the personal values of the organization's leaders.

Second, the chosen core values must be described in the context of the business' daily life. Everyone involved should clearly understand what behaviors they prescribe and proscribe. The greatest meaning emerges from passionate dialogue that continues until shared agreement is reached. Short-changing this definition process will result in vague, vapid values that may impress some people when they are hung on the walls, but will have little value in shaping desired attitudes and behaviors.

What's in a word?

Words can have different meanings to different people. For example, the word "garden" may conjure up a variety of different images depending on a person's experiences and perspective. One person might think of neat rows of vegetables. Another might picture flowers in full bloom. A third person may visualize the majestic gardens of Versailles. Because one word can have very different meanings, a crucial part of the definition process is describing in detail what each value represents.

In his book *Joy at Work: A Revolutionary Approach to Fun on the Job,* author Dennis W. Bakke talks about how the company he co-founded and led as CEO defined its shared values. One of the chosen core values proved to be especially challenging to describe.

"When (we) first used the word 'fun' to capture the kind of

working environment we wanted to create," said Bakke, "(we) never could have guessed at its layers of meaning. It forced us to think through exactly what was meant by 'fun' and the best ways to explain it."

Bakke's company eventually defined the core value "fun" to mean rewarding, exciting, creative, and successful. They also defined what "fun" was not. This definition process, which they went on to apply to each of their values, has continued year after year, so all employees are increasingly clear about what every value means in a practical sense.

When a company has clearly defined its core values, decision making is efficient and straightforward. That doesn't mean that every decision is easy, but it does mean that most decisions, even the most difficult ones, are clear.

Thinking 360°

An entrepreneur, with whom I was working recently, had defined three values to shape his interactions with customers: excellence, transparency, and generosity. He never thought, however, how these values might apply to other aspects of his business. At the time, he was soliciting support from developers and investors. Although he needed the contributions these people would bring to his business, he admitted that he had been rather guarded in his discussions with them because of concerns about confidentiality. In the process of defining his core values, he realized that he needed to apply the value of "transparency" to all his interactions, not just to his dealings with customers.

After he changed his approach and became more open and candid with the potential investors, they were able to give him more useful recommendations, and he was better able to assess their intentions. The shared values of "excellence" and "generosity" became a central component of their dialogue, which enabled both sides to feel more comfortable about entering into a business relationship.

John Faulkner, president of Cornerstone Solutions, a $25 million dollar landscaping services company, likes to keep things simple. His guiding principles—vision, value, and victory—all begin with the letter "V" because it makes things easier to remember.

The same principle applies when defining your core values. They don't need to be complicated to be meaningful, but they do need to be understood. Clearly defined core values are the strong foundation and unifying fiber of successful organizations.

~ Questions for Reflection ~

- Are your organization's core values clearly defined, reduced to writing and integrated with your vision and mission statements?

- Do the people in your company understand what behaviors reflect your core values?

- Do they understand what behaviors do not?

ChappellRoberts

ChappellRoberts is a branding, advertising, marketing, and public relations agency founded in 1978 by Deanne Roberts. From its headquarters in Tampa, Florida, the firm serves clients in a variety of industries throughout the southeastern United States. Colleen Chappell is president and CEO.

Owning our values

Before I joined Roberts Communications in 2002, I was jetting around the country for a Fortune 100 company, with all the perks and VIP passes you get working in Corporate America. I believed I had it all. Then my sister died unexpectedly from complications from diabetes.

As I walked out of the hospital, I said to my brother-in-law, "I have sold my soul to my career. I've got to make a change."

I was really too exhausted and sad to do anything, so I just said to myself, "God will work it out."

I had been a client of Roberts Communications for many years, and Deanne Roberts had been my mentor since college. Around the time my sister died, Deanne happened to ask me if I'd like to join her for dinner.

Over dinner, she said that although this was a difficult time in my life, she wanted to talk to me about an important business matter. She said that after ten years of soul searching, she believed I would be the one to ultimately continue her legacy as head of the agency.

It was the perfect opportunity presented at the perfect time. So I took what many believed was a huge leap of faith. I gave up tens of thousands of stock options and walked away from a very secure and lucrative position.

I remember when I resigned, my boss looked at me—he was a great guy and a mentor, too—and said, "Colleen, people do not resign from these positions, especially when they are at the top of their game and moving up. Are you sure?"

I said, "I really can't explain it, but I'm 100 percent sure." It was a gut instinct that I couldn't describe, but it's turned out to be the best decision of my career.

Every day has worked out to be something better than I dreamed for my career, as well as my family. The time I've had with my family is priceless and the financial rewards continue to grow.

From the first day of our partnership, Deanne and I were grounded and aligned about how to run the business. We had complementary skill sets. With positive growth every year, we nearly tripled our staff and doubled our revenues. It was an incredible ride, one that I couldn't have imagined for myself.

Defining our values

We have what we call the ChappellRoberts Manifesto. It defines who we are, what we represent, and our intentions about the future. It illustrates how we will work together and tells the market why we should be chosen over other agencies. All our team members and clients know what they can expect from us.

Our mission is to create positive change by building strong brands that deliver enduring value.

Our vision is to be a recognized creative force sought after by clients who value a fully integrated, strategic partnership with an ensemble of passionate people.

Our guiding principles are as follows:

- *We serve our clients with an exceptional level of quality and dedication.*
- *We value our long-term reputation more than short-term gain.*
- *We act with honesty and integrity as individuals and as an agency.*
- *How we achieve results is as important as the results themselves.*
- *Our work environment stimulates fresh ideas, creativity, and fun.*
- *We work together as a team, respecting each other's contributions and valuing differences.*
- *We each take personal responsibility for our actions.*
- *We put ourselves in the shoes of others and seek to understand before being understood.*
- *We communicate openly and constructively, and resolve conflict for mutual gain.*
- *We continuously learn and improve, treating success and failure as opportunities for growth.*

Our mission, vision, and values affect every part of the agency and every client relationship. We've set the bar very high in terms of brand management, creative, and client services.

Sharing our values

We strongly believe in living our core values on a daily basis. They're posted on our walls so you see them as you walk in. Every employee has signed them. We consistently talk about them in weekly staff meetings.

They are in all of our employee manuals and planning manuals. Whenever we conduct employee evaluations or performance agreements, we talk about how we are living or not living our core values, as well as where we need to improve to ensure they remain our sustainable foundation.

We actively share our manifesto, our mission, our vision, our guiding principles, and our brand promise with all of our team members, clients as well as prospects. Like the Good Book and the Ten Commandments, our core values are simply about doing the right thing in business and, more importantly, in life.

Institutionalizing our values

When I came on board, one of the first things I did was implement a formal performance agreement process. It has three parts, all weighted equally. We ask each person the following questions:

1. *How well have you adhered to the agency's core values?*
2. *How much have you contributed to the agency in terms of productivity and new business?*
3. *How much have you contributed to the community?*

Most agencies judge performance by profits and new business. We are very different in our approach and it has paid off. In our performance agreements, profitability generated by an employee is only one-third of a larger equation.

Rather than forcing all employees to concentrate first and foremost on new business development, we take into account their unique skills in light of the culture of our agency. That frees us to utilize their talents where they can be of maximum benefit. It also keeps us from doing another thing that's common in the agency business, which is selling clients things they don't need.

In a performance evaluation, if an employee has saved a client money and built a stronger client relationship, even at our expense, we reward the employee because we know that it's in our best long-term interest. They are living by our core value of not seeking short-term gain at the expense of long-term reputation. In other words, we have built value-based incentives into our model.

We reward community service because we believe in giving back to the community. We also promote service because our people are creative, and they need an outlet. The more of an outlet they have, the more energized and creative they will be, and that benefits our clients. It's really a win-win. We incorporate community service into our structure as well as into our culture.

We've also institutionalized our core values into our hiring process. I firmly believe that the most important decision I can make is who to bring onto our team. In the last phase of every interview, I pull out our core values. I talk about our performance agreement and why we weight the three parts equally.

A job candidate, who says he can't live up to our core values, or who shows during the interview process a lack of respect for our culture, is absolutely the wrong choice. We are passionate about our core values. Right from the first interview, every employee we now have on staff has expressed sincere gratitude for the emphasis we place on core values. They want to be part of an organization that holds the value bar high.

Although I stretch our employees, I remind them that I won't let them fail. I tell every employee, "If you live by our core values, any mistake you make is forgivable. Just learn from your mistakes and don't make the same one twice."

Many of our employees have fallen down and made mistakes, but they didn't break core values. We coach them and help them move to the next level by leveraging our strong core value foundation.

Honoring our values

Whenever I make an important decision, I start by asking, "How does this fit with our core values?" About 99.9 percent of the time that leads to a direct answer. Core values are not really that complicated if you stick by them.

It is critical that our employees know, understand and honor our core values. We allow people to make mistakes, but certain things are not acceptable. We have had to terminate employees when our values were compromised. These were not decisions we took lightly because people and their families and well-being were impacted. They were also difficult decisions because of the disruptive ripple effect the terminations would have throughout the agency.

When I communicated these decisions at our staff meeting, I would tell them, "I want to let you know that I terminated an employee today because he broke a core value. Every one of you has signed on to our core values. When we stand in front of our clients, we promise to live up to them. I, as the leader of this agency, cannot say that we have core values if we don't live up to them all of the time, regardless of whether others are looking."

Everyone knew that terminating an employee was going to have a definite, immediate impact on the production of our agency. But when I told them the plan of action, I think there was a huge sense of pride that we would stand up for our beliefs.

Our clients respected us for this as well. When we had to notify our clients about letting an employee go, one of them said, "I wouldn't want to be you today." But, I told him, "It's *not really that hard. Our core values were broken. It's the easiest tough decision we've ever made."*

Although these decisions were disruptive in the short-term, the agency has flourished since then. More importantly, our clients and our employees have witnessed how we really live by our core values, and that's strengthened the culture of our organization.

During the economic downturn, a client wanted to take down all their billboards and shut down their entire outdoor campaign. It was past the cancellation deadline, and most agencies would not have cancelled the media buy. We stood to lose a lot of money, but we worked diligently to get our client out of the commitment. Two months later, that client came back and doubled its media buy.

It's just the law of giving. I've seen it over and over again. People call it a leap of faith. I don't think it's a leap; it's just a daily step. Do the right thing, and it will come back. That client needed to get out of a really big financial commitment. We could get them out, so we took the hit. We are their partner and now they trust us more than ever because that's how we operate.

I've told clients not to launch a large-scale marketing campaign until they have their internal operations running more efficiently. Even though the recommendation risked the client pulling the campaign permanently, it was the right thing to do. There aren't many agencies that would do that. But why would we encourage a client to run a campaign when it's not going to be well executed? That would be just wasting their money. We have to spend their money as if it is our money.

Honesty builds our longer-term reputation, and people really appreciate it. Our goal is to develop a true trusted-advisor relationship. When we are a trusted advisor, we're at the top of our game. It's not about transactions, but trust.

Beyond ethics

I attended a speech by the former CFO for the State of Florida and she said something quite profound. Someone asked her why so many businesses were in ethical trouble. She answered, "Years ago, people would sit around the boardroom table and ask, 'Is that ethical?' Slowly they started to move toward, 'Is that legal?' Now, some people have moved to, 'Will I get caught?'" Those are very different philosophical questions.

At a recent staff meeting, we talked about a competitor who chose to represent what turned out to be an unethical client. They made a lot of money, but they also took a big hit to their reputation. That client could have been ours if we didn't focus on one of our core values—"We value our long-term reputation more than short-term gain." For us, the risk simply outweighed any financial reward.

You have to be very careful about how you grow. Could we triple our size now earning more money? I would venture to say we absolutely could. But we're doing it the right way with our eyes keenly on the long-term and based on core values. Honoring our values has proven to be key to creating a sustainable business.

The value of core values

One of the toughest challenges of our agency career occurred when my business partner was unexpectedly diagnosed with a rare, aggressive cancer. It was a devastating blow to our team. We had to find strength to walk this journey together and we found it in our core values. I remember going into the staff meeting and saying, "I don't know how we're all going to get through this but we will—together. There's a reason we are all here together at this point in our lives."

We bound together tighter than ever as a team through all this adversity. We leaned on our faith and on our core values to show the world that as a team we would not just survive anything we faced—we would thrive in the face of any adversity. This would be our tribute to Deanne and her legacy at the agency.

The dividends from core values are not just in money, but in peace of mind. I can sleep at night over every decision I make no matter what the business impact because they were made based on our core values. There is a sense of peace that becomes a guiding force. It's really empowering. I feel for people who don't have that because it's hard enough being a leader. It would be impossible for me to lead this organization if I didn't have my faith and our core values to lean on. Making decisions based on core values will ultimately pay off in dividends. I know that because we've lived it.

Sharing Core Values

"Next to doing the right thing, the most important thing is to let people know you are doing the right thing."
~ *John D. Rockefeller*

Chapter 7 – Sharing Core Values

Whenever I return from the nursery with my car loaded with new plants, I'm eager to plant them and watch them grow into the beautiful garden I visualized when I bought them. For a week or two I'm excited about my project and encouraged by the results. Then, I'm embarrassed to admit, the rest of my life usually takes over and my commitment dissipates.

Too many business leaders are like that when it comes to core values. They return from a strategic planning retreat excited about the core values they've defined. They call a company meeting and announce them to the rest of the organization. They may even post them on the company's intranet, display them on wall plaques, and print them in their employee handbook. Then they move on to the "more important" task of running the business.

I call this the "if we tell them, they will follow" approach. It doesn't work. Without consistent communication, core values, like vegetables in a garden that's inconsistently watered, will die on the vine.

For my garden to grow, I regularly have to prune, water, weed, and fertilize. I can't do these things just once and expect the plants to thrive.

Likewise, core values must be continuously and consistently promoted using multiple channels and techniques. Any good marketing executive knows that repetition increases impact. The same is true when communicating your company's most important message: core values.

A half-hearted attempt to promote core values is not just ineffective; it's detrimental. When you have identified and defined your company's core values and don't share them, the message comes through loud and clear that they're unimportant and irrelevant.

Creativity sells

Marketing gurus know that creativity increases the impact of a marketing campaign. Communicating your core values is a form of marketing, so it pays to be creative.

Barbara Sealund is the founder and CEO of Sealund and Associates, a creator of e-learning games and simulation solutions for Fortune 1000 companies and other organizations. The instructional design methodology of their serious games and game engines greatly enhances the effectiveness of traditional training curricula. So I wasn't surprised to learn that she incorporates a little fun into sharing core values.

Our core values are trust, service, and quality. We've posted them on our website and we've built them into our day-to-day operations. One way we promote teamwork and our values is through off-site adventures. For instance, we've taken whole days off to go to Busch Gardens. In addition to having fun on the outing, we have goals.

The goal of our last outing was to come up with creative ideas for our serious games. That was the whole adventure. We went around as a group through Busch Gardens having fun, eating food, and stopping occasionally to brainstorm.

Throughout the day, I would tap people on the shoulder and ask, "What's our vision statement? What does our mission statement mean to you?" If they gave a good answer, I'd give them a gift I'd bought at the park's gift shop. I do that back at the office, too.

For these outings, we'll print up our vision and mission

statement on business-size cards. We will have different graphics depending on what our adventure is. Last time when we went to Busch Gardens, we printed a jeep and giraffes on the front. On the back, was a lion which relates to our mission to glorify God with integrity and quality.

Successful companies conduct onboarding training for every new employee. But companies that truly live by core values know that promoting core values cannot just be part of new employee orientation. It needs to be an ongoing process, so they incorporate core values into all technical, human resource, marketing, and sales training activities to help employees appreciate their importance and understand how they affect daily activity.

The CEO of a civil engineering company gave wall posters and wallet cards to every employee with re-worded versions of the organization's core values. He personalized them by replacing the word "we" with "I" to remind all employees that living their core values is not someone else's responsibility.

Word-of-mouth

Word-of-mouth marketing—creating a buzz around a company's products or services—is the most valuable type of promotion. Effective leaders employ the same technique with core values. They talk about the company's core values in meetings, training sessions, at lunch, and in the break room. They refer to them when they're making decisions, conducting performance evaluations, approving budgets, coaching employees, and developing plans.

For these leaders, talking about core values is as natural

as talking about the weather. They are constantly thinking about their core values because core values are the foundation of their individual identity and the identity of their business.

But it doesn't stop there. Successful leaders also model core values. Words unsupported by actions are hollow. Core values must be caught as well as taught; they must be modeled as well as mouthed.

Thinking outside the box

Promoting core values internally is only one side of the coin. Core values should also be communicated in word and deed externally to suppliers, customers, investors, and others. Sharing core values with the outside world establishes the firm's identity and reputation, and it helps to attract customers, vendors, and other resources who share the organization's values.

Recently I noticed an online job posting that incorporated values in this manner. Following a brief description of the job were the following words:

Candidate will conduct himself or herself in alignment with Company Core Values of Integrity, Trust, Honesty, Teamwork, Accountability, and Quality.

This one short sentence increased the probability of attracting candidates who will fit the company's culture, while discouraging those who don't share the company's values from applying for the position.

Another company promoted its values externally when it announced its new Channel Partner program:

Aligned with our core values of Passion, Accountability

and Relationships, we are focused on building long-term profitable relationships with our channel partners and bringing new value-added partners into the program.

By this external communication of its core values, this company establishes the foundation of the relationship it is seeking with the type of partners it wants to attract.

Every organization must share core values internally before they are promoted externally. But also the promotion of core values externally reinforces the communication of values internally. By sharing them with customers and vendors, employees are reminded of their values and the need to live up to them every day. When employees know that the outside world is holding them accountable to the company's core values, it strengthens internal commitment.

Tending to business

An organization's culture, like a garden, needs constant tending. It's not enough to own and define core values. They must also be continuously shared internally and externally, in words and deeds, through a variety of channels. As with any other marketing program, the message needs to be clearly focused, creatively presented, and frequently repeated.

~ Questions for Reflection ~

- When was the last time you mentioned your company's core values in a meeting?
- Do you formally and informally promote your core values on a regular basis?
- Are your employees involved in promoting values internally and externally?

The Fechtel Company

The Fechtel Company designs and builds high-end, high-quality custom homes. The company also develops residential neighborhoods, smaller office buildings, and office parks. Jay Fechtel founded the company in 1988 and is the CEO.

Owning our values

When I started the business, I wanted to operate with integrity, strive for excellence, and build meaningful relationships along the way. These were my values, but they weren't well developed for my company.

In the beginning I had a mission statement, but I didn't have core values. As we operated for several years, I realized there were things that were important to us in the business, so we began to put them on paper and bring some definition to them.

We're very passionate about doing things with excellence, operating with integrity, impacting people, and having good relationships. I don't think anyone else in our world of custom home building can do it quite as well as our team of people. And this is simply because our values intersect with what our clients want. They want excellence, straightforwardness, and to be treated with dignity, respect, and care.

Defining our values

Our mission statement is to bring honor to God and to have a positive, life-changing impact on people. We want to be the best custom home building company we can be by striving for excellence in all we do, focusing on our processes, and completing projects well.

We also seek to operate with integrity. If we make a mistake, we're going to fix it. We want to be open and transparent with our employees, clients, and sub-contractors. And we want to develop meaningful relationships along the way.

Our core values break down according to the pieces of our mission statement:

- *Treating people with dignity and respect*
- *Being straightforward in all of our dealings*
- *Seeking excellence in design and construction quality*
- *Being sensitive to client and team member needs*
- *Paying attention to detail and doing things accurately*
- *Striving for efficiency and effectiveness*
- *Communicating clearly*
- *Promoting key goals of commitment and cooperation*
- *Promoting personal and professional growth*
- *Following through on promises*

Some of our values have come out of our failures. For example, the value of treating people with dignity and respect came out of my failure to develop meaningful relationships with the people in the company. This is one of our supreme values from which several others derive. When I've messed up on that, our unity and morale has suffered.

There are a lot of opportunities to cut corners in construction, so we really need that value about excellence to help keep our focus right. I don't sleep well at night if we've compromised on quality.

Sharing our values

Right now we have about ten employees who work in the field and seven who work in the office. We do our own craftwork to control the quality, but for the most part we subcontract our work. We call our employees who work in the field our "special forces." They help us keep our high standards for painting, carpentry, cleanup, and other construction tasks.

We use a lot of subcontractors, and for the most part they've bought into our higher standards because they've seen the success of it. If they don't fit with our core values, they don't last long. I continually tell our subs that they will do better in the long run if they follow our philosophy. We don't do a lot of priced-based bidding with different subs. We try to get one or two quality vendors who buy into our values because they are an extension of us. If they are out of character with who we are, it will cause us to be out of character. That can't happen if we're to be successful.

Most of our subs have adopted our values and have seen the benefit of it. Many of their project managers aspire to be like our project managers. They see that our guys are successful and they want to be like that. It's a leadership thing that has been fun to watch. We put three or four bright orange placards on every job site that bullet-point our key values. They inform our subs and everyone else who visits job sites what we're about.

Twice per month we have a luncheon for all of our employees, where we talk about our core values, as well as other things going on in the business. We also let everyone in the company know what feedback we've received from clients, vendors, and others. The feedback is almost always positive, so it's a very encouraging time.

93

A big part of the luncheon is devoted to sharing. We invite team members to share stories about how they've seen fellow team members living our values. The stories are affirming and encouraging; many of them are heartwarming.

For example, at a recent luncheon one of our team members told a story about a fellow team member named David. David takes a sincere interest in the subcontractors on our job sites. He regularly asks them how they're doing and how he can pray for them.

One day David went over to talk to the guy who was there to clean the port-o-potty. We normally don't have any interaction with these people. They come at random times and do their work. You know how seedy a port-o-potty can get. It's a lot of work to keep them clean.

Well, this man was extremely moved by David's offer to pray. It turned out that his son has Down syndrome. He and his wife have been struggling with this issue for years. From then on, several people in our company started checking in with this man and praying with him whenever he was on site.

We know he appreciates it because we now have the cleanest port-o-potty in the state. I'm talking about clean! He scrubs those things down and put these tablets in them that make them smell great. You can smell the fragrance twenty feet away! When you're consistently thoughtful and gracious, people bend over backwards to help you when you need it.

Our people do a lot of community service projects on their own time—putting roofs on houses, helping with repairs, and other similar charitable projects. When we hear of a need, they volunteer without hesitation.

Recently, some of our guys encountered a lot of bugs in a

house they were renovating. One of them called an exterminator and paid for it out of his own pocket. That's the kind of people we have!

We share those stories at our luncheons. It lets everyone know how we're making a difference in other people's lives by living our values. We focus on affirming and encouraging each other.

Institutionalizing our values

We have a distinctively Christian culture in that our mission and values are derived from Biblical principles. Because over the years we've emphasized our mission statement and our core values, we've attracted people who identify with those values. Those who don't identify with them don't seem to want to stay around. They either don't like it here, or they feel they don't fit.

For example, if someone doesn't care about trying to have good relationships with others, they'll feel like a square peg in a round hole. That has made us a pretty cohesive team with a like-minded view about how to do our work and serve clients.

We discuss our mission statement and core values with every person we interview. I ask all job candidates if they have a problem with any of them. I never get a negative answer, but sometimes people say, "No, everything looks fine." Those people probably won't fit.

Other candidates say, "Wow! I've been looking for a company like this. I love everything about your values, and I really like what you're doing." Those are the people who usually end up being successful hires.

One of our values is to promote the personal and professional growth of our team members. Often I tell people on the front end during the hiring process, "If you don't want to receive feedback and grow so you'll be even better at what you do—if that's an uncomfortable thing for you—you will not be happy here." There are some people who just don't want to change. They don't last long in this company.

Our values are important for our clients, as well as for our employees. Building a custom home can be stressful. Sometimes the psychological, physical, and financial pressures strain marriages. Our clients want and need a home builder who will listen to and care for them, someone who has relational skills.

Most of our clients are very concerned about their costs. Sometimes they want to competitively bid their project. But most of our work is not competitively bid. We focus on providing great value at a reasonable price. We don't have the lowest prices, but you can't get our level of service at lower prices.

That's one reason why we can't do high volume. Otherwise we'd end up with a lot of administrative and warranty costs due to the inability to spend time with clients and their projects. Things would get out of control quickly.

Early in my career I was very tempted to price certain jobs low to get the work, and I was tempted to price other jobs higher because I was more confident I would get the work anyway. But as I thought about it, it didn't feel right or fair to price equivalent jobs one way to one client and another way to another client.

So I decided to price our houses fairly and consistently, with a reasonable margin, taking into account the service and other aspects we offer. If that worked for prospective clients, then that was great. If not, then it must not have been meant to be.

This was a step of faith that helped me see that God would provide for us if we did what was right. It took a huge burden off of me, and ever since then we've followed that policy.

We don't use fixed-bid painting contracts for the interiors of our homes. Instead, we pay our painters on a time-and-material basis. We know from experience that if we subcontract that work on a fixed bid, we don't get the quality we must have. We enforce our core values by the way we structure our contracts.

Honoring our values

Suppliers give commissions, rebates or "kickbacks" to builders on some items they purchase for their clients. Or they have "gross" billings, where they send two invoices: one for the builder and another one that shows a higher price, which the builder will use to invoice the client. Often clients don't know that the builder is making money on these purchases.

We don't do that stuff. Unlike a lot of builders, our billing process is transparent. We say right up front that we don't get any commissions, rebates or "kickbacks." We charge our clients at our direct builder cost, and I tell my suppliers to feel free to share that information with my clients.

A few years ago, the supplier of a water softening product set up the contract with our purchasing department so that we got a 10 percent future credit or discount on every unit. I didn't know about it. He charged us the regular price on his invoices, but we built up credits on his accounts throughout the year. At the end of the year, the supplier wrote us a check for the credit amount.

I knew that in our paperwork we promised our clients we wouldn't mark-up supplier invoices. At first it happened innocently, and I didn't do anything about it. I kept putting off dealing with it. Then I started rationalizing that I might as well keep the credit.

After all, the transactions were old and our invoices to clients reflected reasonable market prices.

Later, however, it dawned on me that I had compromised on that part of our values that says we will be fair and straightforward in all dealings. So I sent checks to all the clients who had been affected, telling them that we had received a credit for their purchases.

We had some positive response from that, although it wasn't overwhelming. But that didn't matter. What mattered was doing the right thing and keeping our integrity. We see the return in other ways.

We haven't done any real marketing or advertising in at least five or six years. People walk in the door or call us on the phone. Our team has developed a reputation for walking the talk, so we've got a lot of clients out there who are pretty strong referrals for us.

While we don't spend much money on marketing, we do often spend money on fixing things that clients don't even notice. For example, we'll send our painter into a place and spend an extra $1,000 making it really excellent, compared to what other builders would do.

Early on, there were many times when we didn't do that, and I wasn't happy with the results. That's why we needed to put that value of excellence on paper. We made sure our project managers knew what that level of quality looked like in the field. Now I don't have to enforce those standards; it's just what our people do naturally.

In addition, we've been a member of a C12 group, comprised of CEOs who are also Christians. This has provided the strongest accountability to operating with a clear mission and core values. Over the long term, C12 companies have proved to outperform the general industry in terms of financial metrics.

Exceeding expectations

We'll go to great lengths to exceed our clients' expectations. On one job recently we ran short of a Turkish marble that's very hard to obtain. It wasn't our fault. The client added some areas to be covered, but he felt we should have ordered more originally.

Rather than argue, we decided to find some stone that exactly matched the stone we had run short of. We knew this was going to be like finding a needle in a haystack. I drove all over the city with sample stones in my car looking for a match, and found nothing.

We started making phone calls and were told that this marble had been discontinued. No one even knew what quarry in Turkey it had come from. This looked like it was going to set us back big time. If we didn't find a match, it was going to cost us about $50,000 to buy all new marble.

I actually believe what solved this problem was a miracle in answer to our prayers. Our procurement manager, who excels at client service, found a guy in Turkey through searching on the Internet and sending e-mails. This fellow said that he thought he could get the marble for us. Of course, that's what every guy in Turkey was saying.

But we took pictures of it and e-mailed them to him, and he shipped us pieces of stone that matched so closely they looked like they came from the same mountain.

We ordered the additional marble we needed, taking a risk on a cash-in-advance transaction. That fellow in Turkey somehow loaded the marble on a boat and got it to us.

The client was thrilled. That's an example of how we will go the extra mile to serve our clients.

Caring for people

A woman in our office is responsible for helping our clients choose their appliances, plumbing fixtures, lighting fixtures, and so on. Whenever she hears about a cooking demonstration that is going to use some of the appliances that clients are considering, she will invite those clients to go with her to that demonstration. She knows that it will be helpful for them to see the appliances in action.

She's always thinking about what clients would like. One reason she's so good at that is because she's a former client of ours. We built her house, so she's been through the process. She knows what homeowners need to think about and what they're feeling.

We go to great effort to communicate clearly with our clients and document change orders so they get done properly. That came out of a need to document things much better as our company grew and increased its level of performance. Now we use e-mail extensively to enhance communication, and also to send visuals or pictures of things we've discussed.

One of our staff regularly sends cards and thank you notes and e-mails to suppliers and subcontractors who have done something above and beyond expectations. As she points out, we don't give people enough positive feedback. We don't often treat them with dignity and respect and encourage them in what they're doing. There is a tendency to focus on problems like missed deadlines or improper work. But we like to say "that was a great job" when possible and appropriate. This encourages people.

Whenever anyone is sick or going through a hard time, we send around a card. Everyone signs it and we send it to them. It's just a way of expressing the love and concern we have for our employees and our vendors.

The value of core values

We're a member of a "Builder 20" group sponsored by the National Association of Home Builders. It's a group of about twenty other high-end builders from all over the nation. The builders in our group range from $4 million in sales to over $100 million.

We share company and financial information with each other, and we've consistently been in the top 25 percent in terms of key measures, such as sales per employee, net profit percentage, et cetera. More than once we've been the top performer.

There are some really successful builders in that group, and some of them have great corporate values. I'm convinced that our core values have a lot to do with our financial success.

There are certain things that people value, like integrity and quality. Deep down, we know that some things are right and other things are wrong. That's ingrained in us; it's how we're wired. The guy who's driven by greed may get what he wants, but inside there will be a sense that something's not right. I maintain that if you don't run your business according to these universal core values, you're not going to be fulfilled.

I've seen business people join the boards of non-profit civic organizations because their lives aren't fulfilled, and they're trying to fill the hole by doing something good. It's not bad to serve in that way, but it doesn't solve the problem.

We're only here in this world a short time. Life is like a vapor. I believe all the things we do in that short space of time have eternal consequences. So it's vitally important that we get it right while we're here concerning what God values, so we can build those values into our personal and professional lives. When we get to the end of our time on earth, we're not going to wish we had made more money. We're going to regret it if we didn't develop *better relationships and do things right. It's all about the future, not about now. God made us to glorify Him. Whether we like it or not, or know it or not, that's what our purpose is. Unless we live for that purpose, we will never truly be fulfilled.*

Institutionalizing Core Values

"Things alter for the worse spontaneously, if they be not altered for the better designedly."

~ *Francis Bacon*

Chapter 8 – Institutionalizing Core Values

Have you noticed how the best looking lawns and gardens in your neighborhood get lots of attention, while the ones filled with weeds get very little care? With gardening, as with most other activities, there's a direct correlation between focus and results. It is not enough to desire a beautiful garden; you also have to establish the support systems to make it happen.

For example, the auto-timer on my sprinkler system assures that my yard will be watered regularly. My calendar reminds me when it's time to weed and feed. And I have the proper tools—an edger, hedge trimmer, rake, spade, shovel— to help me do the work. Without these tools and procedures, no matter how much I desire a beautiful garden, I won't succeed.

The same is true for core values. They need supportive infrastructure in order to thrive. Owning, defining, and sharing core values are all essential, but alone they're insufficient. You can have the best definitions and the best intentions; you can sincerely own your core values and promote them aggressively; but if you don't integrate them into your company's operations— if you don't institutionalize them—they will have little sustained impact.

Left hung out to dry

When an organization's policies, processes, systems and procedures aren't aligned with its core values, the company's employees frequently get caught in the crossfire. That happened recently when I called a company to get a rebate. The customer service representative cheerfully answered the phone, "Thank you for calling XYZ Company, where customer service is our top priority!" After I explained that I had been a customer of this company for more than five years and that I earned a rebate under their loyalty program, she proceeded to give me the following runaround:

> *"Yes, I see that you are in fact due a rebate, but it's not my decision. Your request will go before our executive committee to review. They meet once a week on Fridays.*
>
> *Because today is Thursday, I won't be able to get your request to them in time. So it won't be considered until next Friday's meeting. Then we'll mail you some paperwork for you to complete. You must return it to us within 30 days.*
>
> *If any part of the paperwork is not completed correctly, your rebate may not be granted. Once we receive all your paperwork, it will take 6-8 weeks for you to receive your payment."*

This rep, like thousands of others in hundreds of companies, was not able to deliver on the core value of excellent customer service because the company's leadership had failed to institutionalize it. Imagine the negative impact on morale when the employee knows what to do, how to do it and yet is prevented from executing because of failed corporate policies and procedures.

Organizations that gain the most value from core values incorporate them into all of their policies, processes, and procedures. They refer to them when hiring and training people, selecting vendors, setting goals, developing marketing strategies, purchasing goods and services, and approving projects and budgets. They institutionalize them so they permeate virtually every aspect of their business.

Safe and sound

Mark Mazur shared with me how core values are incorporated into daily operations at MJM Electric:

Our values are faith, family and work, in that order. I don't want a company that's so complicated or so big that we don't have time for faith and family. At work, safety and quality are our priorities.

We implemented a safety committee several years ago. You can't make safety a priority if you don't have a process to address safety concerns. The safety committee is a group of employees who are closest to the issues. They meet, discuss, analyze, and make recommendations to improve safety.

Whenever there's a decision to be made, we have five questions we want our people to ask: Is it ethical? Is it moral? Is it legal? Is it in the best interest of the customer? Is it in the best interest of MJM?

Everyone knows we need to get "yes" answers to all of those questions, or we'll change the situation until we do. When my people come to me with questions about what we should do, we run down that list.

We just had a safety and general practices audit by our biggest customer. They brought three guys in to do the audit. They left here so impressed with our culture, the quality of our people, our organization, and the way we document things. I don't deserve the credit for that.

We've got great people who take responsibility for their parts of the business. They are self-motivated and they do their jobs.

No substitution

Tom Strickland, president of Suncoast Team Services, has made it a priority to institutionalize core values into his design/build business:

Most of our business is negotiated rather than competitively bid. When you bid on jobs, you have to invest a lot of time and money, and you're doing really well to get one out of ten. But because of our reputation, we get a lot of referrals and repeat business, which don't require conventional bids.

In tough economic times, being known for integrity is a real asset. When bonding requirements are getting tougher and contractors are going out of business, people want to do business with contractors they can trust.

We let our subcontractors know what we expect of them and when we expect it. To make their jobs easier, we make sure the job sites are well organized and that the projects are well coordinated. A lot of subcontractors will tell us, "We love to work for your company. You guys are the most organized people we work for. Please call us when you have another project in our area."

When jobs are completed, we ask our subcontractors to fill out a questionnaire telling us what we did well and what we need to do better. They give us honest answers because they know they can trust us. You'd be surprised how many say, "This survey is a great idea. I wish every general contractor would do this."

We also have an internal data base, sort of a blog, where our project managers put comments about our subcontractors. When we're putting together a team for a new project, the new project manager can refer to that. It helps him select the best subcontractors for that particular job.

Because we have a good reputation that we've earned over a number of years, good subs make a strong effort to come to work with us. Others don't want to work with us, and we don't want them to.

Core values affect the types of people you will hire, the types of business opportunities you will pursue, the types of vendors you will choose, and the kinds of funding and investment partners you will accept. They attract and repel like a magnet. People who share your values will want to do business with you, and that's good for your business. People who don't share your values won't want to do business with you. That's also good for your business.

Focusing on the customer

Craig Sturken, former president and now chairman of the board of Spartan Stores, told me how his company integrates values into day-to-day operations:

We own and operate about one hundred supermarkets, twenty gas stations, and fifty pharmacies in Michigan and Ohio. In addition, we distribute more than 40,000 private label and national brand products to approximately 350 independent grocery stores.

When I joined the company in 2003, we defined our core values. We argued back and forth about the priorities. Many of us felt that integrity should be number one. But we realized that customer focus has to have top priority. The other values—integrity, valuing people, teamwork, innovation, and accountability—all support customer focus. They're synergistic.

Customer focus affects how we price merchandise, what we sell, when we sell it, where we place it in our ads, and even where we place it in our stores. It drives all our decisions.

We lay out our stores so they're focused on our customers. For example, the most popular milk items are displayed in end caps, right across from the express checkout. We also sell some bread and eggs there. That's for the convenience of our customers who are in a hurry. We don't want them to have to go all the way through the store to get to those items.

We also put soft drinks up front because they are what our customers want. Next to milk, soft drinks are the number one item in our customers' shopping carts. We also do it so our customers can put their soft drinks at the bottom of their shopping carts, where they won't crush their other groceries. Other grocery stores put soft drinks in the back, so they draw customers through their stores. They hope customers will pick something up on their way to get to the soft drinks. Interestingly, the profit margin on soft drinks is much less than it is on milk or anything else, so they deserve to be at the back of the store. But if we're truly customer focused, this is the right thing to do.

Sturken gives core values much credit for his company's

profitable growth. It's evident that Spartan Stores takes core values seriously because they're embodied in the structure of the organization. They impact every aspect of operations, even the layout of stores.

Core values are living organisms. They live in the hearts and minds of people. Like my garden, if they do not receive regular attention, they will wither and die. To sustain the required degree of attention, core values should be woven into the fabric of the organization so that every department—human resources, finance, information technology, sales, marketing, manufacturing, and administration—operates in alignment with them.

~ Questions for Reflection ~

- Can you point to systems and processes in your organization that support your core values?
- Can you identify where your systems and processes interfere with living by core values?
- Are you willing to invest to make a change?

Rutgers Painting

K evin Sheridan founded Rutgers Painting in 1992, immediately after graduating from college. In its first year, with Kevin and two summer employees, the company generated revenues of $40,000. Today it employs approximately 150 painters, six sales representatives, and ten office staff year around. Annual revenues are in excess of $7.5 million.

Starting from scratch

While I was a student at Rutgers University, I painted houses in the summer. After graduation I thought, why not do this for another year? So I recruited two guys, and we painted about ten houses that summer. Then I spent the winter traveling to Europe and Central America.

When I came back, I started getting calls from people who wanted their houses painted, and from workers who wanted summer jobs. So I decided to continue the painting business for another year or two.

Almost before I knew it, we were painting year around. Sales went up to $3 million, then to $5 million, and then to $7 million. It all happened so quickly, I was overwhelmed. Fortunately, I hired an excellent man who helped me set up the systems to run the business.

The lifespan of painting companies is usually one to seven years. They get a lot of business if they're good, and then they can't manage the growth. It's unusual for a painting company to last ten years, but we've been around almost twenty.

Owning our values

It was easy for me to think about core values for my business. I discovered early on that building trust by keeping your word was good for business. From the beginning, I built my company on the idea that I would develop trusting relationships with my customers.

Ironically, only later did I realize that I was making a mistake by not doing the same thing in my personal life. When I was younger and dating, I would think, "I'm a guy. I don't have to be on time. It's okay if I change my plans quickly." But I later realized that I was creating a lack of trust in all my relationships. When I started living my word, I created trusted relationships in my personal life as well as in business.

Defining our values

So our main core value at Rutgers Painting is to do what we say we're going to do. That's it in a nutshell. We believe in keeping our word.

We're also a center for helping people get what they want. We are constantly asking our clients how we can help them. If they want something, we'll try to provide it. If we can't, we'll point them in the right direction. As a company, we also try to help our fellow team members the same way.

Another of our values is to help people become the best they can be. That might not always look pretty because it requires accountability. For example, if someone is slacking off, we want the people around him to say, "We don't want you to get fired. How can we help you do a better job?" If that doesn't work, we want them to go to his manager.

If someone has a 1:00 p.m. meeting and doesn't get back

from lunch until 1:15 p.m., I want five people to call him on it. We maintain that kind of accountability for each other. It's verbal, and it's pretty much a continuous thing. I want to be held accountable too. I invite everyone in the company—painters on up the ladder—to review my performance. I ask them, "Where am I falling down?"

Sharing our values

For our first ten years, we only communicated our values verbally. Now that we're bigger, we post our values and print them in the training manuals we hand out. In meetings, we give examples of people living their word. We talk about our core values openly.

It's difficult for people to understand the importance of taking full responsibility for living their word. It took me a long time to understand that keeping your word creates relationship. So we constantly work to instill this value in our people. When people break this value, we call them on it. We don't just let it slip by.

One Friday afternoon I had to leave early and I asked a guy in the office to make sure the numbers were put back up on a house we were painting. This client was having a birthday party for their little boy that Saturday, and they needed the numbers up so guests could find their house. He said, "No problem. I'll get them up."

When I came to work on Monday morning, I found out that the numbers had not been put up. The client's guests couldn't find the house, and the pizza guy didn't know where to make his delivery.

When I confronted this person, he said, "Oh yeah, I'm sorry," then he went on with whatever he was doing. He obviously didn't understand the importance of building trust in relationships. So I called him on it.

We have to constantly teach people the importance of keeping their word. We give our painters examples so they know when they live their word and when they don't.

Institutionalizing our values

Because we've grown so fast, instilling core values has been a struggle. Our core values were always lived by the managers and the office and sales staff, but they never got down to the painters.

At one time, our painters were mostly subcontractors. But they failed to do what they said they were going to do, and they started cutting corners. When I was supervising the work, we always put two coats of primer on. But the subs put just one coat on if they thought it looked good.

We weren't supervising closely enough, and we didn't realize what was happening until we started getting complaints and noticed a drop in referral calls. It takes a couple of years for the negative word-of-mouth to catch up to you, so you don't notice it at first. In one year we had $250,000 in warranty claims on revenues of about $7 million. I expected warranties to go up as our revenues went up, but I knew this amount of increase wasn't right.

So we switched from subcontractors to employees. It was a difficult and expensive transition because of the workman's compensation and other costs. But we had to do it to live by our values. We've noticed a positive difference in the quality. It's better today than ever.

It's against our core values to hire illegal immigrants, so we bring seventy guys up from Costa Rica every year. They're on visas from the United States government. *A lot of illegal immigrants work in the painting business. Our core values help us avoid that big liability.*

We warranty all our work for three years. If clients call us with a warranty issue, we are out there within a week. If the work wasn't done right the first time, we'll fix it no matter how much it costs. Some companies try to get out of as many warranties as they can. They hire people and make that their full-time job. But we don't operate that way. Our philosophy is to say to our clients, "What can we do for you for free?"

We have about fifteen tough clients who give us the most problems. We go back to them every year to see what needs to be done. We don't wait for them to call us. We visit their houses and offer to fix things we notice are wrong if they want us to. High-quality work has made us successful. As long as we continue to do quality work, we will continue to be successful.

We've had people call us to do warranty work, and we never painted their house in the first place. Some other painters had done it. We had always operated on the honor system in the past, and we didn't have the paperwork systems to keep track. Now we've corrected that.

We actually started a maintenance program because people got angry with our warranties. We were setting the wrong expectations. We would say, "We will paint your house and do the best job on the market. You'll have to repaint in about six to eight years. If there's anything that goes wrong in the first three years, we'll come and repaint."

When something went wrong during the first three years, our customers would get angry. They'd call and say, "We've got problems with your paint job. Come and fix it!" With old houses especially, it's not unusual for the paint to flake, peel, and stain a bit.

117

So we changed the way we presented our warranties. We started telling our customers, "We did the best job we could painting your house, but here's what you can expect. Over time, you'll be getting a little peeling and maybe a little staining. Under our maintenance plan, we'll come back and fix it free for the first three years. After that, it's wear and tear and it's on you. You will probably need to repaint in six to eight years."

After we changed our approach, we noticed a big difference. When the paint stained or peeled, our customers would call and say, "This is just what you said would happen. We need you to come fix it." Because we were living our word, they weren't mad.

Honoring our values

We get about 50 percent of our work from word of mouth. Another 20 percent comes from lawn signs, and about 15 to 20 percent comes from advertising. We used to get close to 100 percent from word of mouth, but as we got bigger, we started doing more advertising.

Our closing rate is about 70 percent, which is very high. That's because most of our prospects have already heard about us. We want our customers to recommend us to their friends before they're even asked. If they happen to meet a friend in the supermarket, for example, we want them to be so excited about the job we've done for them that they'll say, "Have you seen our new paint job? Rutgers Painting did it!"

When that happens, we've passed what I call the "supermarket test." Whether we've painted a mansion or simply a side of a small house, we want our clients to be so satisfied they'll say, "You guys are amazing!"

Sometimes customers try to take advantage of us. A while

back a customer called us. We had only painted one side of these people's house, and they were thinking we had painted another side that didn't look good. But we will go and paint just about anything and consider it under warranty, even if it was someone else's work or a four-year-old paint job.

One lady who had just moved into a house called and said, "You painted this house and it's all peeling." We had painted it for the previous owner 3½ years before, and the three-year warranty had expired. But we didn't have any clause that said warranties were not transferable, so we repainted the whole house for her. That cost us about $3,000.

I did that because it wasn't painted right the first time. Maybe the guys painted it in wet weather. I could tell the peeling wasn't due simply to wear and tear, and I felt we had to make it right. She was kind of a tough client, and she wasn't even that appreciative. But if you keep doing business the right way, people will get who you are.

You are what your business is. You can't hide. If you're in business long enough people will see through pretenses. It took me a while to learn that, but I did. One of our goals is to be profitable, and we take that seriously. But we don't let our desire for profits diminish our commitment to our core values.

As I was visiting a job site not long ago, I noticed that the sanding tool the guys were using was damaging the wood. The woman of the house was irate, and for good reason. By the time I got involved, she had a lot of distrust for our company because the guys weren't delivering what we had originally sold her.

So I spent about three weeks trying to solve a very delicate situation. She had questions about every step we took because she wanted to make sure we didn't screw up. In the end, the back of the house wasn't looking right. Her husband asked me what we were going to do, and I told him we were going to replace it.

119

We had bid the job at $4,000, and our original cost estimate was $3,000. At this point, we had already spent about $7,000 in labor and materials, and it was going to cost us almost $5,000 more to replace the back of the house with new cedar. But we went ahead and did it. The job ended up costing us about $12,000, so we lost $8,000. A contractor friend said I was crazy. But I don't blame those people. I would have been upset if painters had done that to my house. I treated their house as if it were mine.

The value of core values

We learned from that experience. I called the manufacturing company that sold us the tool. Their factory rep came down to New Jersey from Maine to show us how to use it. Now we have strict regulations to prevent that from happening.

That woman is a tough client. I'm not sure if what we did will ever come around to help us. She said, "Ultimately you did a great job. It was a tough experience, and I can't say that I will recommend your company. I will definitely recommend you as a person, though, and I'll tell people the whole story."

But do you know what? I got a Christmas card from her— the only Christmas card I got from a customer. It's a wonderful Christmas card with her son's picture on it. It was all worth it. And if I see her, she will greet me because I took care of her. They have no idea we lost $8,000 on the job. They think we only lost about $4000.

I use that Christmas card story with my guys. I remind them that problems are our opportunities to be heroes. When we get away from our values, that's when we get into trouble.

Honoring Core Values

"The superior man understands what is right; the inferior man understands what will sell."

~ *Confucius*

Chapter 9 – Honoring Core Values

Clear definitions, effective communication, and comprehensive support of core values are all necessary. But in the final analysis, actions speak louder than words. To be authentic, core values must be lived.

Honoring core values can be challenging. Just as a keel places a sailboat in dynamic tension with the wind, core values place an organization in dynamic tension with the prevailing winds that swirl about in the world of business. There will be times—many times perhaps—when disregarding core values will seem like the most prudent thing to do.

When honoring core values requires terminating a key employee or turning down an alluring business opportunity, even well-intentioned leaders can waiver. They justify compromising their core values with rationalizations such as efficiency, productivity, profitability, survivability, or even worse, "Everyone does it." Failure to honor core values is worse than failure to have them. Such hypocrisy undermines respect, creates confusion, damages morale, and destroys trust.

True core values are non-negotiable

"This note is legal tender for all debts public and private." Those words, printed on all paper currency of the United States, turn mere pieces of paper into valuable currency by making them negotiable.

Core values, however, work the other way around. They only have value when they're non-negotiable. Your non-negotiable commitment to core values will be tested time and again. You can count on it!

Tom Strickland, CEO of Suncoast Team Services, told me about such a test:

> *A few years ago, we finished building a facility that had a lot of glass in it. The cleaning company we hired did a horrible job; they left scratches over about a third of it. One of our core values is quality, so I told the client, "We're going to have to replace this glass." The client said, "Why not just give me the $75,000 that the new glass will cost you. You don't need to spend the labor to install new glass."*
>
> *A ton of work was involved, but I said, "No, we're going to replace the glass because somewhere downstream I don't want you looking at that defective glass and saying, 'I can't believe I let that guy write me a check instead of putting in the right glass.'"*
>
> *The cleaning company failed to acknowledge their liability, so we took the $75,000 out of our pocket and spent our labor to change this client's glass. That was an easy decision to make. We can earn $75,000 somewhere else, but we only had one shot to earn our reputation with that client. Of course, he's going to share that story many times with others, which in the long run will help us.*

Suncoast Team Services is committed to honoring core values at all times and in all situations. Their values provide non-negotiable guidance for decision making.

Accountability supports faithfulness

Accountability strengthens commitment. Without account-ability, day-to-day pressures can easily override an allegiance to core values. Internal accountability is vitally important, but it's only half of the equation. Just as companies use internal and external auditors to preserve financial integrity, organizations need internal and external accountability to safeguard their commitment to core values. Boards, auditors, peers, and other types of accountability partners provide detached objectivity that will help the organization stay true to its values.

The C12 Group offers this type of accountability for owners, CEOs, and presidents of businesses. The goal of this organization is to help leaders achieve excellence in their business and personal lives. Participants meet regularly in small groups for mutual edification, encouragement, and accountability.

Scott Hitchcock, the facilitator of The C12 Group in the Tampa Bay area, shared how external accountability works in his forums:

> *In our groups we talk about how to live according to Biblical principles, with the view that God owns everything in our lives, including our businesses. As we discuss these things, from time to time members of the group will realize they need to make changes in the way they do a few things, and the other members of the group will encourage them.*
>
> *Sometimes, some people who need to make changes in their behaviors balk when things get hard. They get caught up in the allure and temptations of the world, and they're not willing to make the necessary spiritual transformation. Other members of the group may confront the person in a supportive way. Most people appreciate this type of accountability because it helps them live their lives with integrity and balance, and ultimately be more successful.*
>
> *Other people say they'll make the changes they know they need to make, but they don't do it. They come back*

with the same problem, or a different problem with the same root cause. So we remind them, "Hey, you know you wouldn't have this problem if you had done what you had said you would do."

We had a situation where a person kept procrastinating. One of the other guys in the group looked at him and said, "I'm not going to give you any more advice. You've been here three years now, and you still have the same type of problems. You haven't done what we told you to do the first two years, so I am not going to waste my time giving you anymore advice. Go fix it and then come back. Quit wasting our time." That guy is not in the group anymore.

All business leaders need this sort of honest and supportive external accountability, but most don't have it because they haven't sought it. Boards of directors are an excellent source of external accountability. However, because many companies recruit board members primarily based on their positions in business or the community, they offer limited, if any, accountability to core values.

In order for a board to provide truly meaningful accountability, its members must be committed to the core values of the organization. Otherwise, conflicts and poor decisions will result as the leaders of the organization try to live according to values the board does not understand or share. To avoid this conflict and enhance the board's effectiveness, commitment to the organization's core values should be a primary criterion for selecting board members.

Sol Pitchon, executive director of New Life Solutions, a Christian-based pregnancy counseling organization, told me how he relies on his board for external accountability:

The board is the rudder of the organization. If you have a weak board, you're going to have a weak organization. We make sure our board members share our organization's values. We don't ask just anyone to be on our board. We check personal and business references.

The members of our board are on the same page because we are committed to the same vision and values. They are people who want to do things with integrity and honesty. Because we are a faith-based organization, they must sign a statement of faith. Most importantly, they must be in love with Jesus.

We have very healthy dialogue in our meetings because, as iron sharpens iron, one sharpens another. We hold each other accountable to living in accordance with our values. If we're wrong, we admit it.

Honoring core values is both the easiest and most difficult thing a values-centered leader will be called upon to do. It's easy because values simplify decision making by clarifying right from wrong. It's difficult because honoring values demands courage and conviction, when we may naturally gravitate toward convenience and compromise.

~ Questions for Reflection ~

- What internal process have you established to assure that you honor your core values?

- Do you have external accountability partners to provide feedback on how well you live your core values?

- What happens when you or someone in your organization fails to honor your core values?

Storr Office Environments, Inc.

S torr Office Environments, Inc. sells office furniture, lab furniture, floor coverings, and related services from four stores in the Southeast. The company has more than 225 employees and annual revenues in excess of $75 million. Tom Vande Guchte is the majority owner and CEO.

Owning our values

My first job out of school was in public accounting, where I got to work with a lot of small businesses. Then I went to work as a general manager of a small business for a few years in Michigan. Later I took a job with Steelcase, the office furniture company based in Grand Rapids. I worked with the Steelcase dealers, who of course are small business owners.

In 1991 Steelcase sent me down to Raleigh, North Carolina, to run a struggling distributor they had recently purchased. It was doing about $8 million in annual revenues, 95 percent of which came from sales of new furniture. Eight months later Steelcase sold the Raleigh facility to me.

Since then we've reduced the number of employees in that store from 225 to 165, and increased revenues from $8 million to about $50 million. Only about half of the store's business comes from new furniture sales because we've diversified pretty dramatically into other products and services.

Over the next few years, we acquired three additional stores: one in Greensboro, North Carolina, one in Tampa, Florida, and one in Orlando, Florida. Every one of them has been a turnaround situation. We've had to challenge our people to do better, set performance expectations, and start measuring.

I know what it's like to be demoralized in a job because you're stagnating and being underutilized. I experienced that in my early days with Steelcase. So we make an effort to engage our people by providing an environment where they are challenged and fulfilled.

That's not always easy to do. Every furniture installer is not going to feel fulfilled in his role. People can make choices early in their lives that limit their options later. We don't have control over that.

When you start changing the culture, people either change or they leave. Typically you don't have to fire them. They feel uncomfortable in the new environment and move on. After five years, only about 50 percent of the original staff is still with us.

Defining our values

From the beginning, we built our core values around three very basic principles. We took them from a Lou Holtz video called "Do Right". The three principles are:

1. Do what's right.
2. Do your best.
3. Treat others as you'd like to be treated.

The first one—do what's right—relates to integrity. We are committed to operating with integrity with our customers, vendors, team members, the government, and the community.

The second principle—do your best—relates to excellence. In all we do, we want to excel.

The third one—treating others as you'd like to be treated— relates to relationships. We care about people and treat them with dignity and respect, without showing favoritism based on position.

Those are our foundational values: integrity, excellence, and relationships. They're easy to say, but it's harder to live them every day.

Sharing our values

One of my main responsibilities as the CEO is maintaining and communicating our culture. The key to doing that is consistency. The leader's actions and words must be consistent. You can't say one thing and do another.

For example, I try to live a pretty simplistic lifestyle. I drive an eight-year-old car because I want to send the message that we're all on the same team and that I'm not any better than anyone else. My kids have washed the company trucks and cut the grass here for ten years, so our people can see that our family has a strong work ethic.

We're not doing everything right; we've got our challenges. But when we screw up, we admit it. We say, "I made a mistake." I don't try to put on a front, because I want people to know who I really am.

I'm a firm believer that you must communicate regularly about everything. In each of our people's minds, there's a big vacuum waiting to be filled. If we don't fill it with the facts, it will get filled with who knows what. So we try to educate, challenge, and encourage people on a regular basis.

Sometimes I don't think we understand or appreciate the importance of honest and consistent communication. I know how much information means to people because I get e-mails saying things like, "Thanks for sharing about that issue. It's good to see our company has leadership that's concerned about it."

131

One way I communicate our values is through stories. Stories are powerful. I tell stories about how we've lived our values. That's not to boast—we've still got plenty of room for improvement—but to encourage and motivate our people to live by what we say.

Here's an example of a story I might tell: We had one customer who cancelled a contract and went with a competitor. About six months later our accounting department informed me that we still had this company's $180,000 deposit.

We went back to this client and said, "It appears you guys have forgotten about this $180,000 deposit you paid us when you started the contract. Here's the money we owe you." They were surprised and appreciative, and they were also a little embarrassed that they had forgotten about it.

A couple of years later, we had a similar case with a vendor. We had purchased used furniture from them and had given them a check for $25,000. About a year later, our accounting group came to me and said, "They've never cashed this check." Obviously they had lost it, so we went back to them and paid them the $25,000. Naturally, they thanked us profusely.

I'll tell you one more story to show how this type of opportunity to live our values comes up on a regular basis. About a year ago we had the roof repaired on our building. The roofing company completed the work and we paid them. However, we subsequently found major installation problems, so we had the credit card company reverse the charge.

It took the roofing company almost a year to fix the problems, and in the meantime they forgot that we had never paid them. I contacted them and said, "You guys have never asked for this $40,000 that we owe you, so here it is."

We share some of these stories with our people so they understand that our values are not just words. If we say we're going to have integrity, we actually have to live it.

Institutionalizing our values

Our policies support our values. We want our people to know how we are doing, so we share our financial results each quarter. We've done that since I've owned the business.

We pay a bonus of 20 percent of all our profits over 2½ percent. It goes to all of our employees, except our leaders and our commissioned salespeople. Both of these groups have their own performance-compensation plans. Each year our administrative staff, installers, customer service reps, receptionists, and so forth usually get between $2,000 and $5,000 each, which is huge for them.

In other ways, we are very conservative fiscally. We have always reinvested all of our profits in the company, so we are in a strong financial position.

We use a team approach in interviewing because it gives us more input for making decisions, and it increases buy-in when people participate in the decision-making process. On my own, I might tend to lower my standards if I'm tired of interviewing and I really need to fill a position. Involving other people forces me to be more objective.

We talk about our core values when we hire people. We want to make sure candidates are a fit before we hire them. But I don't try to force my personal faith on anyone. We hire people from all faiths.

We pray before company meetings. I tell the people, "I'm not here to offend anyone. I do this because I personally believe we've been tremendously blessed, and I want to acknowledge that blessing by thanking God for it." Then we pray briefly and move on.

We have a corporate chaplain who comes in once a week. He walks around and talks to everyone in order to build relationships so when people have a need, they will feel comfortable talking with him. He's available to our people 24/7 to talk and pray about finances, family issues, or whatever. It's a confidential relationship, and it's been a very valuable thing for our people.

As best we can, we want to help our people to grow professionally, spiritually, emotionally, and physically. We have programs in each of those areas, like the chaplain program I mentioned. Ultimately, growth is up to the individual, but I'm disappointed that we haven't done more in helping people grow.

We have a strong emphasis on customer service—on treating others the way we would want to be treated. For more than ten years we've measured customer satisfaction. We track it, and we pay bonuses based on it.

For example, we send out customer surveys for every job over $5,000, and we make a $25 contribution to Habitat for Humanity for every survey that is returned. If our combined customer satisfaction scores exceed our goal for the quarter, we pay a bonus to all team members. In addition, we pay a bonus to all of our salespeople when the customer satisfaction scores for their specific customers exceed our goals.

Honoring our values

Several years ago a customer placed a fairly small furniture order with us, for about $50,000. After we delivered it, I got a phone call. The customer was furious. "Your guys damaged our tables when they delivered them. We want them replaced at your cost right now!"

I went over and looked at the tables. Most of the issues were really minor. You would get that kind of wear in a week of normal *use. But they insisted that we replace $10,000 worth of tables.*

Keep in mind, our industry is not highly profitable. The average office furniture dealership makes about 2 percent before taxes or about 1 percent after taxes. On a $50,000 order, our profit was projected to be only about $5,000, assuming no returns.

To make matters worse, these tables were made to order, so we knew we were going to have to resell them to someone else at way below our cost. We stood to lose quite a bit of money on the deal. But we went ahead and took the tables back because we wanted to live our core values and doing the right thing.

Interestingly, a couple of years later that customer bought $500,000 of furniture from us. They told the salesperson that if we had refused to take those tables back, they would never have done business with us again. I share these stories with our people to show how we stand behind what we do.

Living your values may not look like the profitable choice in the short term. But over the long run, I believe it works out for the best. I can't tell you there's always a direct correlation between living our values and good things happening, but it happens a lot.

Here's one story that makes a more direct correlation. A computer software company—it was rather small at the time—asked us to quote on a service project. We gave them a quote of $7,000. After some time went by, I got a call from this customer: "Your people said that because the project is taking longer than they estimated, they need to charge us more than the original quote."

It turned out that we had simply underestimated our costs; there'd been no change in the scope of the project. So even though we stood to lose a considerable amount of money, I said, "It was our mistake. We've made a commitment and we're going to keep it."

The value of core values

Over the years, as that software company has grown, they have spent more than $5 million with us. If we had backed away from our commitment that day, I'm convinced they would have taken their business elsewhere. Some people might say, "Well, you were lucky." To me, it's a consistent theme of being rewarded for doing the right thing.

I don't view our company as a family. I call it a team because everybody is expected to contribute. We all have to live our values while we are adding value. If we're not successful as a team, we won't have a team.

We had a manager whose performance was not where it needed to be. In a meeting with him, when we were talking about the lack of results in a certain area, he spent a lot of time telling us about all of the ways he'd been caring for his people.

I said to him, "I want to make one thing very clear to you. How we treat employees is very important. That's one of our core values. But that's not a substitute for performance. We expect you to get the job done."

A lot of people equate Christianity with a warm, fuzzy environment. That's not what we are. We want to equip people, give them a chance, and help them grow. But if someone is not succeeding, it's bad for them and bad for the organization. They don't get the rewards of success, the job doesn't get done, and the rest of the team has to pick up the slack.

I believe God designed work as an opportunity to experience rewards and fulfillment. If that isn't happening, we need to help the person move on to a job that's a better fit. Some people would say that's not being compassionate. They equate compassion with compromise.

I'm a firm believer that you don't have to reduce profits in *order to live your values. This is not theory to me; I've experienced it. Living by Biblical principles is the key to being successful. If I take care of my customers and my people, the profits will come. Doing the right thing works.*

Living Core Values

"A business that makes nothing but money is a poor business."

~ *Henry Ford*

Chapter 10 – Living Core Values

In the preceding chapters, successful CEOs shared their perspective of the value of core values. Their businesses represent a number of different industries. Some are small and others are relatively large; some are privately owned, while others are publicly traded. Nevertheless, all of these leaders share one thing in common: In spite of typical fears and struggles, which they readily acknowledged, they have remained firmly committed to their values.

Every organization operates by a set of values. Your customers, your suppliers, the citizens in your community, and others who are familiar with your company know what your values are. The question is, are the values they observe the ones for which you want to be known?

Positive core values must be cultivated. The CEO, with the collaboration and buy-in of other leaders within the organization, must take responsibility for defining, sharing, institutionalizing, and honoring them. In fact, I would argue that cultivating core values—first individually and then organizationally—is the primary responsibility of the CEO.

Where do you start to create a winning culture?

I have a GPS system in my car that will tell me how to drive to a destination if I simply enter the address. But the final destination alone is not enough. Before my GPS can tell me the route, it first must know my starting point.

Business planning is like that. If your "destination" is to consistently live by core values, you must assess where you are now before you can begin your journey. You must identify your strengths and your opportunities for growth so you can point yourself in the right direction.

On my website *www.thevalueofcorevalues.com* I've provided self-assessment tools to help you assess your current situation. Use them to determine how well you and your company incorporate your core values into hiring, performance evaluation, decision making, leadership development, and other aspects of your daily operations.

Employee surveys are another useful tool you may want to use to gain a clearer picture of where your people stand with respect to owning, promoting, institutionalizing, and honoring your core values. I suggest categorizing your responses according to the respondent's position in the organization (e.g., executive leaders, managers, and employees or finance, marketing and operations) so you can spot any real or perceived gaps that may exist in awareness, understanding, and commitment.

Excellent companies regularly utilize these types of assessment tools to reveal blind spots and guide their improvement efforts. Make self-assessments a regular part of your business improvement process. When you know where you are, you can better figure out how to get where you want to go.

Implementing the Five Keys to Values-Centered Leadership

 Owning Your Core Values

Many of the CEOs highlighted in this book derived their core values from their faith. Others arrived at their values experientially or by some other means. Regardless of how they arrived at them, they all have well-defined values to which they tenaciously hold.

In contrast, many other people—perhaps most people—wander through life without a written set of core values that define how they choose to live. Their actions are dictated more by feelings, circumstances, and financial considerations than by values. The lack of a firm foundation complicates their decision making and hinders their progress. It becomes easy to rationalize poor choices and difficult to make right ones.

On my website, *www.thevalueofcorevalues.com*, you'll find an exercise to help you identify the values or principles that are most important to you. List some important decisions you made in the past. What principles guided you? With the benefit of hindsight, would you do the same thing again? If not, what would you do differently and why? Write down your answers. Use this exercise to begin to formulate a list of standards or beliefs that influence your behavior. Rank your values, with the values you consider to be non-negotiable at the top of the list.

Keep your list in front of you for a month as you make decisions to determine whether you really consider these values to be valid guiding principles. If you violate a value without regret, it's almost certainly not a core value. Continue reflecting, reviewing, and refining until you have identified the non-negotiable principles upon which your life is based.

 Defining Your Core Values

The process of defining core values is best accomplished through a collaborative effort involving the appropriate people within your organization. Persist until you have shared agreement and total commitment. You're going to have to live by these values, so take as much time as you need to define them clearly. If your values are vague, people will be forced to guess what they mean, and they're likely to guess wrong.

You may choose to begin the values-definition process at a weekend strategic planning event, but don't plan to complete it there. Continue to challenge, review, and refine the results in subsequent weeks. Keep pressing forward until you've identified a set of values that engenders everyone's commitment.

Once you've identified your core values, define them fully in terms of workplace behaviors. Detail the specific behaviors that do and do not correspond to each. Be clear about what types of infractions would result in termination.

Consider soliciting input from your entire organization using employee surveys and facilitated workshops. Facilitating can be as easy as listing each value on a flip chart in the format shown below, handing out markers, and inviting team members to fill in the blanks.

Core Value	
We *DO* live this value when we . .	We *DON'T* live this value when we . .

Remember, you haven't really defined your values until you've described their acceptable and unacceptable behaviors in detail. To see examples of how other companies have defined their values, visit my website *www.thevalueofcorevalues.com*.

Defining core values is an on-going process. As different situations involving values arise, you will need to refine the meaning of your core values so they remain explicit and pertinent. As your people assume new roles, they will need to rediscover how core values should influence their behaviors and the success of the organization.

Your organization will never outgrow the values-definition process. Florida Hospital, for example, is more than 150 years old, but in 2007 the organization significantly clarified its values by adding extensive descriptions. At a minimum, you should periodically review and refine your core values as part of your strategic planning process, to ensure that they are current, appropriate, and clearly understood.

 Share Your Values

Once defined, core values must be instilled in the minds and hearts of your people so they are shared and lived by all. That requires consistent, effective communication in word and deed.

Effective communication requires thoughtful planning. The plan may be simple or complex, depending on the size of your company. But one thing is certain: regardless of shape, size, industry, or type of organization, communication must begin at the top. It also must extend beyond your employees to your suppliers, customers, and other key stakeholders.

The most successful leaders communicate organizational core values at every opportunity. They make values an important component of their conversations when they roll out new programs, reward or discipline employees, announce decisions, address customer complaints, and take other important actions. Consistent communication tied to specific events clarifies the meaning of each value and highlights its importance.

Naturally, core values should be presented and explained in the company's employee handbook, but that's only a start. Every day of every year, goals should be set and performances should be assessed and rewarded with reference to the organization's core values. Employees should gain increased understanding of and respect for them throughout their careers.

How do you know if you're doing a good job communicating your core values? One way is to randomly ask employees to name them and to explain what each value means in terms of everyday behaviors. Accurate answers more than likely indicate effective communication. If they're unsure about what the core values are and what they require, it's time to ramp up your efforts.

Another way to assess your communication efforts is to ask at the end of every day, "How did I reinforce our core values today?" During regular leadership or employee meetings ask your team, "What have you done to reinforce our core values since the last time we met?" Positive answers to these questions usually indicate that you're doing a good job of communicating core values.

Don't leave sharing your core values to chance. As with any other marketing program, promoting values requires focused, persistent attention.

Institutionalize Your Values

Weave your core values into the fabric of your organization. Review all human resource policies, quality control procedures, marketing practices, compensation and rewards arrangements, decision-making processes, and other components of your operations to make sure they incorporate your core values. Ask questions such as the following:

- How do our information systems support living our values?

- Do our customer service systems encourage our employees to serve our customers well, or do they promote efficiency and economy at our customers' expense?

- Do our budgeting processes motivate all departments to develop plans that support our values?

After examining all of your systems and procedures, make the necessary upgrades to support your values. Start with your employee-hiring processes. Develop procedures, interview questions and checklists that will help interviewers and others identify candidates who share your organization's core values.

Don't allow the pressure to fill positions cause you to compromise on your hiring decisions. Studies show that long-term employee success depends much more on cultural fit (sharing the company's values and beliefs) than on knowledge and skills. Make the necessary investment to find the right people and you will be rewarded with increased productivity, lower turnover, and fewer headaches.

In recommending that you consider personal values and character in your hiring decisions, I am not suggesting that you apply rigid criteria that limit diversity. Rather, look for people of good values and character that fit the culture of your organization.

In his bestselling book *Uncommon: Finding Your Path to Significance*, former NFL coach Tony Dungy describes how he built winning football teams by refusing to compromise on character. His organization's player-evaluation forms have a category labeled "DNDC." That stands for "Do Not Draft because of Character." Tony says, "For me as an employer, how you do your job has always been more important than what you do."

How true! To grow any successful organization, it's not enough to hire people who are willing to live by your core values because they know that's what you expect. You want people who are excited about living by your organization's values because they know that's the right thing to do. During the selection process, do more than simply ask candidates whether they agree with your company's values. Frame your interview questions and conduct your reference checks to solicit examples of how candidates responded or would respond in certain situations involving values. Past patterns are good indications of future behaviors, and ultimately of character.

My garden lies under some mighty oak trees. When I visit a nursery, the plants that require full sun are so colorful that I'm tempted to buy them. But that would be a mistake because they wouldn't survive in the shade.

Companies face the same kind of temptation when they consider hiring a candidate who has an impressive résumé and conducts a brilliant interview, but who doesn't fit the company's culture. To alleviate this temptation, institutionalize core values into your hiring processes.

Once you have defined, communicated, and institutionalized your core values, expect people to live them. Over time, as you adhere to core values, those who don't fit will be weeded out, either voluntarily or involuntarily. Conduct this process with even-handed persistence and patience. An orchard does not grow from a seed overnight.

 Honor Your Values

Values-centered leadership demands a non-negotiable commitment to core values. Rationalizing decisions that violate core values is the first step toward undermining trust and respect for you as a leader and your company as a whole. Deviations from values may start small. Like a snag in a sweater, they initially may be barely noticeable. But left unchecked, snags can unravel until the sweater is unattractive at best and non-functional at worst.

If you take core values seriously (and that's the only way they should be taken), a time will almost certainly come when you will need to terminate an employee for violating them. Decide in advance what types of violations of values warrant termination and what types merit additional training or coaching. If your leadership team has trouble reaching shared agreement, assess why. Are your definitions unclear? Is your resolve lacking? Are the values you've identified truly core values?

For a variety of reasons, some companies are reluctant to terminate employees who violate core values. Some leaders simply shy away from conflict. Others are afraid of the potential fallout, especially if the employee has close relationships with customers and other employees or has hard-to-replace skills. Still other leaders, out of an overabundance of compassion, will put up with undesirable situations in hopes that things will work out or that the offending individual will change. Such patience and compassion can be good qualities, but they need to be balanced by consideration for the overall good of the organization.

Leaders that fail to take decisive actions when core values are violated set themselves up for failure. When an individual violates one or more core values, the other employees almost always know about it. If no action is taken, employees lose respect for the leadership. The failure to honor core values causes confusion, breaches integrity and violates trust. Morale and productivity take a dive. Keeping an employee on the payroll that is out of step with the organization's values is not only unfair to the rest of the organization; it's unfair to the employee. He or she will be better off working in a more compatible environment.

That's why it's essential to make sure everyone is fully committed to living the core values from the beginning, before they are put to the test. Determine in advance what types of violations warrant dismissal, and follow through with whatever you decide when tests arise.

In his book, *Stolen without a Gun: Confessions from Inside History's Biggest Accounting Fraud – The Collapse of MCI WorldCom*, author Walter Pavlo, Jr. describes how his rationalization of core values landed him in federal prison. The transgressions started small and kept growing, until at the end of an eight-year period he pleaded guilty to obstruction of justice, money laundering, and wire fraud. When I met with Walt, he told me that he lost his ethical bearings when Ralph McCumber, his first boss and accountability partner, took another job. Perhaps because he didn't have well-defined values of his own, Walt depended on Ralph's positive influence to guide his behavior.

To guard against compromise in your company, establish an accountability structure that starts at the top. Honoring core values requires conviction and courage, reinforced by accountability.

Really successful businesses are led by confident leaders who welcome open, honest dialogue. You've met many such leaders in this book. They believe in holding others accountable and they are willing to be held accountable.

Shared core values help make accountability possible. When all of the members of an organization are accountable to the same standards, mutual accountability—up, down, and across the organization—becomes natural, objective, and supportive. When shared values are absent, accountability can become threatening, subjective, and confrontational. Honoring your core values means striving to adhere to them more perfectly. Perfection is impossible, of course, but striving for perfection at all times is eminently practical. Continue to improve by honestly admitting mistakes and diligently looking for areas that need improvement.

My garden needs to be consistently checked or the weeds will take over. Likewise, core values need constant attention, or they'll cease to be honored. The process is unending, but the rewards are unlimited.

The Value of Core Values

"Real riches are the riches possessed inside."

~ B. C. Forbes

Chapter 11 – The Value of Core Values

Core values require time and effort to define, promote, and institutionalize. To honor them, your policies, procedures, and actions almost certainly will have to rise above the common practices of your industry. You may at times have to pass up opportunities your competitors will accept. So why bother with them at all? Do the benefits really outweigh the costs?

Yes, I am convinced that over the long run living core values drives increased market share, revenues, profitability, morale, customer satisfaction, and all of the other traditional measures of success. I've seen this correlation validated time and again. All of the leaders I interviewed for this book have experienced it.

Living by core values won't exempt you from economic downturns, troublesome personnel issues, unreasonable customers, or other challenges. In fact, doing so will sometimes expose you to additional risks and short-term disruptions. But over the long run, adherence to values will allow you to weather these and other storms with calm confidence. You will be more likely to prosper because you will be operating within a solid framework of right priorities.

Values and customers

Many of the companies I wrote about in this book do little or no advertising. They don't need to because they get most of their new business from referrals. The leaders of these companies testified about the benefits of treating customers in accordance with their core values.

Although they often had to make short-term sacrifices to honor warranties, accept customer returns, and take other "right" actions, the additional business and other benefits that accrued over the long run far exceeded the original costs.

Your customers ultimately will clearly recognize what you truly value. If you value integrity and service, that message will come through in your dealings with them. They will reward you by continuing to buy from you and encouraging others to do the same. On the other hand, if you primarily value your own profitability while merely giving lip service to the values of integrity and service, your customers will eventually get that message too—and take their business elsewhere.

The value of loyal customers and loyal employees

Honoring core values increases trust, trust increases loyalty, and loyalty is good for business. Satisfied customers will return again and again to purchase your products and services. They'll stick with you, even when you occasionally slip up, and they'll refer new business to you. Studies show that companies with high levels of customer loyalty typically grow revenues at twice the rate of their competitors.

Customer loyalty increases profit margins. By some estimates, it costs five times as much to attract a new customer as it does to retain an existing one. Companies with low customer turnover have more time and money to serve their current customers and attract new ones.

A company that retains loyal employees builds an experienced, dedicated, and productive workforce that can deliver the high level of service necessary to cultivate loyal, satisfied customers. On the other hand, a company with high employee turnover is at a competitive disadvantage because it's estimated that replacing an employee costs on average one to three times the annual salary of the employee. Disgruntled or disengaged employees that remain on the payroll can curtail productivity, damage morale, and create personnel problems that consume management's time and energy.

What if ...?

Perhaps you've been asking yourself, "What if core values don't work for our company? If it turns out that they hurt our profitability, can we go back to the drawing board?" If these thoughts are strongly on your mind, you need to better understand what core values are. Core values are not merely tools for running your business; they are the foundation on which your organization rests. They are not simply prescriptions for what you should do; they are descriptions of who you are.

You don't simply choose core values based on whether you think they'll work; you choose them because they're what you really believe. Questions about the efficacy of values can indicate a lack of clarity about what you cherish. If you're nagged by such questions, consider digging deeper to see what's really at the "core" of who you are and what your business is about. When you hit solid bedrock, where true values reside, questions of expediency tend to fade away.

What's the value of core values?

Does adherence to core values always result in maximum profits? As you have read in the stories recounted in the preceding chapters, sometimes it doesn't—at least in the short term. When you're in the midst of a values-based decision, you can never be sure of the financial outcome. Although I'm convinced that living your core values promotes sustainable profitability over the long term, maximum financial rewards are never guaranteed. Although I'm all for profits, it doesn't work to honor values for the sake of tangible rewards alone. You must be willing to hold fast to your core values regardless.

By definition, values reflect what you believe is "right," not merely what you think is "useful." If you try to live core values based on their usefulness, you will toss them overboard whenever they seem to be "unreasonable" or "impractical." Disposable core values are not really core values at all. They're simply policies, and somewhat flexible ones at that. True core values, on the other hand, are beyond compromise. They are so fundamentally a part of your company's identity that you will not deviate from them—ever!

All of the leaders in this book talked about the non-monetary rewards of living their core values. Several called these intangible benefits "priceless." Sleeping well at night, having the satisfaction of knowing you've done the right thing, experiencing the joy of introducing a person to Christ, enjoying a sparkling clean port-a-potty, or receiving a Christmas card from a difficult customer you've treated as you would like to be treated—these are all practical examples of priceless rewards.

Although I firmly believe that living core values promotes maximum business success—and my definition of business success includes profitability—I've observed that organizations that benefit most from living their core values tend to define success in light of their values. They're working for rewards that are substantially greater than profitability alone.

I encourage you to find out for yourself how valuable core values can be. I believe your company will be more prosperous in tangible terms. But even more important, I believe you will grow to appreciate that the greatest value of core values is ultimately in the values themselves.

Acknowledgements

A lot of people have a book inside of them that they're just itching to get out. That was not my situation. I've never wanted to write a book, and I never thought I would. But sometimes our goals change, and what we once thought was impossible comes to be. Since you're holding this book in your hands, you can tell that's what happened to me.

This book, I believe, is the result of a divine inspiration. That's the only way I can explain it. The thought emerged clearly in my head one day: "You are going to write a book about companies that are successful because they live their core values, and you're going to use case studies to write this book." Along with this vision—and just as important—came the passion to pursue it.

I've had a lot of help along the way and without the prayers and support of many people; this book would not have been possible. At the risk of leaving someone out, I'd like to especially thank:

- Michael J. Dowling – my talented writing partner/editor who took my thoughts and words and helped transform them into the book you have before you. *www.michaeljdowling.com*

- Cover design: Todd Engel, *www.toddengel-engelcreative.com*

- My business partner, Mary Owens, who lives the principles of values-centered leadership.

- The business leaders, some of whom you've met in these pages and all of whom volunteered their time and shared their stories: Bart Azzarelli, Greg Celestan, Colleen Chappell, Peter Cunzolo, John Faulkner, Jay Fechtel,

Christa Foley, Terry Hedden, Roy Hellwege, Jason Herndon, Scott Hitchcock, Mark Mazur, Walter Pavlo, Jr., Jay Perez, Sol Pitchon, Barbara Sealund, Kevin Sheridan, Tom Strickland, Craig Sturken, Tom Vande Guchte, Laurie Watts, and Tom Wolfe.

- The many people who reviewed the manuscript – Dr. Michael Nastanski, Imelda Butler, Matthew Kelly, John Faulkner, Carl Bennink, Glenn Henderson, Chuck Bengochea, Kerry Loeffler, Mark Galvan, Joan Jansen, Susan B. Huetteman, Jim Wilson, Al Huetteman, John Grant, Jill Pearson, Pat Dominguez, Kristen Allman and Lorraine – and prayed for me as I wandered along this journey.

- Scott Huetteman and engage360 for the design and layout of this book. *www.engage360.us*

Most importantly, I want to thank my loving husband, Scott, who encourages me daily, and my brilliant daughters, Katie and Abby, who are always there to inspire me.

References

Chapter 3

Mark Mazur
President and Owner
MJM Electric, Inc.
www.mjmelect.com

Chapter 4

Orlando Jay Perez
Vice President Mission and Service Excellence
Florida Hospital
www.floridahospital.com

Chapter 5

Roy Hellwege
President and CEO
Pilot Bank
www.pilotbank.com

Tom Strickland
President
Suncoast Team Services, Inc.
www.suncoastservices.com

Peter Cunzolo
President and CEO
ExecuJet Charter Service, Inc.
www.execujetcharter.com

Chapter 6

Joy at Work: A Revolutionary Approach to Fun on the Job, by Dennis W. Bakke Copyright © 2005 by Dennis W. Bakke

John Faulkner
President / Chief Visionary Officer
Cornerstone Solutions
www.cornerstonesolutionsgroup.com

Colleen Chappell
President and CEO
ChappellRoberts
www.chappellroberts.com

Chapter 7

Barbara Sealund
CEO
Sealund and Associates Corporation
www.sealund.com

Jay Fechtel
CEO
The Fechtel Company
www.thefechtelcompany.com

Chapter 8

Craig Sturken,
Chairman
Spartan Stores
www.spartanstores.com

Kevin Sheridan
President
Rutgers Painting
www.rutgerspainting.com

Chapter 9

Scott Hitchcock
Tampa Bay C12 Chairman
C12 Group
www.c12group.com

Sol Pitchon
Executive Director
New Life Solutions
www.newlifesolutions.org

Tom Vande Guchte
CEO
Storr Office Environments, Inc.
www.storr.com

Chapter 10

Uncommon: Finding Your Path to Significance by Tony Dungy, Copyright © 2009 by Tony Dungy.

Stolen without a Gun: Confessions from Inside History's Biggest Accounting Fraud – The Collapse of MCI WorldCom by Walter Pavlo, Jr. & Neil Weinber, Copyright © 2007 Etika Books LLC.